101 Facts That'll Convince Your Liberal Friends To Walk Away

by
Tyler Zed and Dylan Wheeler

E4L Publishing, United States of America

Copyright © 2018 by Tyler Zed and Dylan Wheeler

All rights reserved. No part of this publication may be reproduced, distributed, or transmitted in any form or by any means, including photocopying, recording, or other electronic or mechanical methods, without the prior written permission of the publisher, except in the case of brief quotations embodied in critical reviews and certain other noncommercial uses permitted by copyright law. For permission requests, write to the publisher, addressed "Attention: Permissions Coordinator," at the address below.

Printed in the United States of America

First Printing, 2018

Cover art: Ben Garrison

ISBN: 978-1-7327315-0-9
ISBN-10: 1732731500

E4L Publishing
PO Box 2585
Baxter, MN 56425
E4LPodcast@gmail.com

FOREWORD

All of the facts in this book are irrefutable proof of the reality we live in today. Everything else written is our opinion and should be taken as such. Every fact in this book is cited in the back of the book with sources. We purposely sought liberal news sources for most of the facts, so there is no refuting the information being given. Why? It's either accept the information or say the information reported on by the liberal news sites is fake news.

Before you read any further, please consider these two facts:

FACT #1: It has been illegal to pay men and women different wages for the same work since the Equal Pay Act of 1963 was passed.

FACT #2: In 2017, only 996 lawsuits were filed under the Equal Pay Act of 1963. 798 cases were determined to have "no reasonable cause," or that there was, in fact, no discrimination.

If you read nothing else in this book, please take to heart these first two facts. They are undeniable truths. Once you accept them, ask yourself how they conflict with the Democratic party's narrative, specifically the wage gap narrative. We will address these facts later.

INTRODUCTION

Truth is an objective thing. We have to keep it that way or our society implodes. When people push subjective truth over objective truth mental illness is celebrated, values run amok, the wrong politicians get into power, tribalism takes over, and we stop moving forward as a country; which is very ironic since "progressives" or leftists are the peddlers of subjective truth but preach evolutionary progression moving humanity forward.

In the society we should be promoting, you don't get to decide as an individual what reality is and isn't. Whether truth is coming out of Donald Trump's mouth or Maxine Waters' mouth, the truth is the truth. The problem with many politicians, and one of the main reasons why I think Donald Trump was elected, is that most politicians weaponize the truth by bending it, and more often than not, pulling the rug out from underneath its objectivity and replacing it with complete lies. Trump bulled his way through the political establishment's proverbial china shop and shattered their lie-telling, truth-bending vote machine. Hell, that was one of the things he ran on, "The Swamp." We've all seen the swamp in action, and he was one of the first ones to run against them.

I'll never forget my first experience with "the swamp" taking advantage of Americans with lies. I was 11 and in gym class when two planes crashed into the Twin Towers. I remember asking my mom after school that day if we were safe where we were in Minnesota (of course she said yes). It was scary for all Americans. At the time our whole country wanted to find out who was responsible and we wanted to retaliate so this tragedy would never happen again. In our vulnerable state, President George W. Bush told us that Iraq had "weapons of mass destruction" and that this tragedy could happen again if we did not take those weapons away. We fell for it. I continued to watch over the next decade as that lie got thousands of Americans killed in the Middle East and wasted TRILLIONS of our tax dollars. All because the president had an agenda and he fulfilled it by lying to us. (You thought I'd have a bias toward everyone on the right, huh? Again, the truth is the truth, and the truth is that George W. Bush lied to us.)

Before we go any further and dive into the facts, let me give you a little background on who we are. My name is Tyler Zed. Together with one of my best friends, Dylan Wheeler, we put this book together because we care about truth and we hate getting lied to by our leaders. We're smart enough to see that by bending the truth and telling lies, politicians can emotionally charge people, and when they emotionally charge people it's very easy to get them to do what you want, a Machiavellian go to.

"Weapons of mass destruction!"

That phrase gets people angry. It frightens them. It's scary. It makes them want to take action. They say exactly what the politician wants to hear, "let's go to war and get these weapons of mass destruction!" The swamp wins.

Manipulating people in a vulnerable, emotional state is a fundamental strategy in politics. Why? Because it's easier to get people to do what you want when they are blinded by anger, sadness or even happiness. Have you ever been in a debate with someone and your point isn't getting across? You are unquestionably right, but they are dancing around the argument and even attacking you personally. What happens? Likely, you feel your blood boiling and your heart racing. That is the feeling of losing control. You retaliate and attack them personally. It's what your debate opponent wants because as soon as you attack them personally, every point you previously made is null and void. Nobody wins.

For example, a boxer in a boxing match or a martial artist in an MMA fight. Why do fighters talk to each other like they do? It's a planned strategy. In the ring, conserving your energy while getting your opponent to waste theirs is a vital part of their strategy. If you bite an opponent's ear or taunt him relentlessly, you break his spirit, and his response will be out of control anger. You fill your opponent with emotion and get him to do what you want, which in this case means a full-on attack and he wastes his energy. Once he is on empty, you can swoop in and defeat him.

Manipulative words have filled the opponent with anger. Are the boxer's words true? Probably not. Spewing lies, bending the truth, and manipulating your opponent are a means to an end: to get him to do what you want.

What's different in a politician? The only difference is that their opponent is the voter. The only thing standing between them and power is our vote. What can they say to attain our vote?

To be clear, I'm not implying that all politicians or people that run for office are swamp people, but we cannot be naive and should approach everything in politics with skepticism. I think Bernie Sanders at one point in his early career may have actually cared about the people he represents, even though his policies are atrocious and would destroy our country. I believe

Rand Paul has goodness in his heart and cares about his constituents. I truly believe Donald Trump cares. If he didn't care about this country, I don't know why he would throw away billions of his fortune while sitting as President. The point is, I do believe some politicians care about their constituents and this country, but history has shown that power corrupts, and in an unbelievably new world of technology, strategies have had to shift to match our new society and LIES are a big part of those political campaign strategies.

Example, the 2016 presidential election.

"Women are paid 70 cents on the dollar." This was a claim spouted by Hillary Clinton and many in the media. At face value, this is an outrageous claim. If the whole country takes it as truth, at a bare minimum 50.8% of the country (which are women) become angry. How unfair to be paid less for equal work! With this statement, the corrupt politician is tugging us with strings toward the voting booth, we are drunk on emotion and completely outraged at the fact that there is a great injustice in our country … at least according to this politician vying for our vote. This politician says they are going to fix it and we get to the booth, and we vote for them because we believe them.

They often win … not in Hillary's case because enough Americans knew that this claim was a complete lie. When digging into her claim that women are paid less, it is clear that it is a blatant lie, or severely bent truth at best (refer to fact #1 and #2).

Another strategy and great lie used to charge voters emotionally is that of identity politics. "Anyone who supports Trump is racist! If you have any pigment in your skin, they hate you!" Immediately, the left garners millions of votes by emotionally charging people on that lie. If you are not familiar with identity politics, it is the practice of separating people by groups. Mostly by race, religion, gender and sexual orientation. Democrats use this as a strategy to gain votes by pitting the different groups of people in our country against each other. Their motto is "divide and conquer." We will cover many of the narratives they use to divide and conquer later in this book.

The military taught me an important lesson about identity politics. There is always a job to do, and it doesn't matter what skin tone you have, what religion you follow, who you sleep with, or what gender you are, that job WILL get done because we NEED it to get done for the good of the military and the country. There's no time for pettiness and thinking about group differences. It does not matter when focusing on the mission. That same mentality needs to apply everywhere, especially in government. There is no time for identity politics. There is stuff to do in our country to make it better, and that doesn't happen when we don't work together. That being said, the prize of peddling social outrage — power — is far too big and too easy for the left not to push it. WE need to see through their drivel and do all of this ourselves because ultimately we are the powerful ones. WE give them the power they have, and WE can take it away at the voting booth.

It seems pretty obvious and transparent that the left's tactics mentioned above are lies, so why and how do people fall for this nonsense when it is so evident that it's not the objective truth?

We think the two biggest reasons for this are apathy and ignorance.

Apathy is the lack of interest or concern.

Ignorance is the lack of knowledge or information.

The two of these qualities combined create something more harmful to a group of people than the black plague.

Apathy alone is just as harmful as a bad idea like socialism. When you show a lack of interest or concern in your job, personal relationships, or in your own well being, your life WILL suck. When you show a lack of interest in the politics and laws that dictate how much you will pay in taxes, what you can and can't say on the internet, what you should and shouldn't eat and where you can and can't travel, your life will suck even more. "My vote doesn't matter, so why even vote?" This is apathy at its finest.

Politics are a huge part of your life whether you care or not, but why would you ever decide to be apathetic and not want to take ownership of this huge part of your life!?

Stand up and be heard, get out and vote, and start living your life like you give a damn! I understand that arguing and trying to find common ground can be exhausting, but it matters. Do whatever is necessary to manage the pitfalls of politics. All I ask is that you take ownership of this beautiful thing we have here in our country. Don't just be a taker of all this country has to give. Be a giver and fighter for the freedom that so many before you have fought for. Do this for you, for your neighbors, for your family and your children. Otherwise, before you know it, there will be no one left to speak for these things.

Ignorance alone is almost as harmful as identity politics. We are all ignorant to a degree. It is literally impossible to know everything. However, when it comes to the responsibility you have with your vote you cannot simply vote for somebody or call yourself a Democrat or Republican because your parents raised you that way, or because one candidate is the same gender as you or has the same skin tone.

That is ignorance to the highest degree.

That is not thinking with your brain. Learn as much as you possibly can, watch every single news source whether you are a leftist or a righty. Learn it all and educate yourself. Do not be ignorant.

Search for hard, objective facts. Facts. Facts. Facts. And more Facts. An opinion is not a fact. The opinions that Dylan and I write under each fact in this book are NOT facts. Donald Trump's opinions on a person are not facts. Rachel Maddow's irrational tears are not facts. Your feelings are not facts.

I say all of this at the start of the book because seeing the ignorance and apathy around us is why Dylan and I started tweeting and making our videos. Too many times before we started all of this we heard, and still hear, "why do you care so much? It's not like your vote matters," or "it's just obnoxious to voice your opinion, especially online."

No, it's obnoxious to sit there like a child, in the middle of the floor while adults are trying to figure out how you are going to live your life. That's exactly what you are if you think like that. You are a toddler in the way. You allow others to decide for you by asking when and what you get to eat for dinner.

Start caring.

Once you decide to do that, read the information in this book and digest all the facts. Go out and find more facts and more information, and take control of what guides your life actions. Apathy and ignorance are cancer, and they will kill you slowly, dragging you into the abyss. Forever forgotten.

Dylan and I put this book together because we care, a lot.

Like many of you, one of the first doses of reality in my life came when I worked for minimum wage washing dishes at a restaurant at 15. I counted up my hours in my head for two weeks, and I had every dollar accounted for on how I was going to spend it. Then the check came and it was almost half of what I was supposed to get after taxes. I couldn't believe it. I had been robbed, I thought. The worst part was that it was completely legal!

As the years went by I started finding out how the other half of my paycheck was being spent. The more I found out, the more I felt the need to say/do something.

My second dose of reality. I was a senior in high school, and Dylan was a junior. We decided that we would each put $100 of our hard earned money into an E*TRADE account (which was stupid of us to begin with, the cost of making a trade was $12. We immediately lost 6% of that $200 the second we made a trade. We didn't see it then, but we learned the hard way). Half of that money went into Fannie Mae, and half of it went into a tiny gold company, UXG. I remember it was football season because we were checking our stocks on our phones after a 2-a-day practice, and we were trying to figure out ways to raise more money for our soon to be outlandishly successful stock trading company. It wasn't more than two weeks later that Fannie plummeted during the housing crisis and a few months after that our gold stock turned out to be a horrible pick.

That experience forced us to figure out the hows and whys of the housing crisis, because of course, we wanted to know what was happening with our money and if we were ever going to see it again. It was very eye-opening and a hard pill to swallow learning about the crisis. That crisis was in large part due to government-backed institutions like the Federal Housing Administration (FHA) backing nearly two-thirds of the 10+ million subprime loans during the great recession. Agencies like Fannie and Freddie were forced to back these bad loans in the name of identity politics. Pushed by who? Liberals on the left.

When Dylan and I found this out, we had to scratch our heads. Why would the left push this? If you can't afford something, how can you be offered a loan? Is our government that stupid to force bad loans? It was a basic principle our parents taught us: If you don't have the money, you can't have it. If you want it, you have to work harder to get more money for it. It really is that simple. Or at least it should be, we thought.

A $100 lesson learned for both Dylan and me, and one of the first political ones that helped mold us and the way we think today.

Having our money swiped by the government in our first ever paychecks and then again during the crisis gave us the ammunition to start speaking up. We didn't want to start making adult money one day and find ourselves in the same position, losing more money. We saw then how apathy let the left get away with their irrational policies and ideals. We couldn't stand by silently and allow this stuff to happen without saying something.

My third dose of reality: The 2016 election.

As we all know, the election was extremely polarizing and energized many to get involved and speak up. Not only that, it was one of the first elections where social media decidedly played a MASSIVE part in the campaigning and debating, not just between the candidates but between every individual, their family, friends, and strangers on places like Facebook and Twitter.

After seeing how leftist policies can ruin a country and steal people's money, and observing the corruption of the left during the 2016 election (DNC rigged elections, extreme vote pandering with identity politics) Dylan and I, like many of you, spoke up on social media. We did our best to spread the truth about these corrupt people in places of high power that get away with anything and everything, like the Clintons. Slowly but surely people started following and paying attention to what we had to say. As I write this, we have over 600,000 social media followers in total. I say this not in a bragging tone, but to show what YOU have put together. Our voice, which is still small, is heard by the people we are speaking up against, and it is because of you.

This isn't our platform, it's yours. We serve you. With this platform, we have vowed to keep speaking the truth about the lies of the left and get more Millennials on board.

Even if we only had 10 social media followers, I would continue to speak the truth, and we believe you all should, too. By doing so, you are taking control of your life, and the things that rule over it, like government. With all of us working together we make a pretty powerful voice and we can use it to defend the truth and make the changes that are needed!

With this book of facts, we hope to shed light on information that maybe you didn't know. With this information, we hope to arm you with more knowledge and ammunition to debate and defend your position in your daily lives and spread truth. All it takes is one powerful fact to open somebody's eyes and force them to dig deeper and hopefully see the world as it actually is, and not through the blinding lens of emotion that can cloud objectivity. Making decisions through emotion can make anyone vulnerable to manipulation. If you only have ten followers, share it all. Maybe one of those ten people will question what they know, and they will begin to dig for facts and information.

We want you to leave this book lying around your house. Maybe leave it somewhere in a public setting after you have finished reading it, or even suggest to a liberal friend or family member to read it if they are open enough to give it a chance. We have a tremendous battle ahead so let's get to it!

ON GENDER

To reiterate the importance of our first two facts, we want to start our first chapter with more on those two facts and more about gender.

Gender is a cornerstone in identity politics, and it is used to pander to Americans for their vote. The saddest part of it all is that most of it is a lie, and while they preach equality and fairness, there is much that is not talked about in regards to men's issues that prove they don't care about "equality" and fairness at all.

Before you delve into this chapter, and the rest of this book for that matter, we are here to expose some of the false narratives pushed in the media and by politicians. We are not calling for a campaign for or against any group of people (in this chapter, men) but these facts force questions on the left that they cannot answer.

The entire Hillary Clinton campaign relied on getting over half the country outraged with the idea that women are treated unequally compared to men. Facts suggest that this is far from the truth.

Laws prevent women from being treated unequally and believe it or not, many hard-working Americans teach their sons to be gentlemen, and gentlemen treat women how they are supposed to be treated — with respect. Women are not objects, women are not beneath men, and they are not treated as such in this country as the left likes to say and would like you to believe. If any man out there truly believes women are beneath men, then he is a pig. He does not represent the majority and don't believe the left when they tell you he does.

Here are some facts about gender.

FACT #1:

It has been illegal to pay men and women different wages for the same work since the Equal Pay Act of 1963 passed.

An entire campaign was run off this lie: "I'm with her"; "Equal pay for equal work"; "women are paid 70 cents on the dollar in comparison to men."

70 cents on the dollar is the worst lie of them all. When you look at the country as a whole (the total wages for all women in America combined vs. the total wages for all men in America combined), there is not an equal number. There are so many explanations for why this is. More dangerous jobs pay higher and are occupied mostly by men (facts on this later), women have children and stay home longer after giving birth or ultimately decide to stay home because of daycare costs. I mean, if men could produce milk from their nipples, maybe it would make sense for them to stay home more often, but they don't. Also, if men are paid more, wouldn't it be smart for businesses to hire all women to save money?

The law is the law, and the Equal Pay Act of 1963 clearly "requires that men and women be given equal pay for equal work in the same establishment." Period. End of story. It's the law.

Do you think you are being paid unfairly based on your gender? If so, shoot us an email or a tweet, and we will gladly help you find a lawyer to take on this injustice because after all, it is ILLEGAL TO PAY MEN AND WOMEN DIFFERENTLY FOR EQUAL WORK.

Under the left's narrative, there must be millions of women that file lawsuits under this law. Exactly how many women have filed lawsuits under this law? Onto fact #2.

FACT #2:

In 2017, only 996 lawsuits were filed under the Equal Pay Act of 1963. 798 cases were determined to have "no reasonable cause," or that there was, in fact, no discrimination. There are roughly 125.9 million working-age women in the United States.

I can translate this statistic in a few ways. There are roughly 125.9 million women in the United States. 996 of them filed a lawsuit for unequal pay for equal work. Percentage-wise that's .0007911% of adult women that claim to have been paid unfairly. When we factor in that roughly 80% of those 996 cases were thrown out, we have a big fat lie on our hands.

Let's pretend that .0007911% is an extremely high number. Has it gotten worse under the abhorrently sexist President Donald Trump?

Nope. Actually, it improved in 2017. According to the hard facts, in 2000 there were 1,270 lawsuits filed (when the population of adult women in America was less), and in 2016 under Obama, 1,075 lawsuits were filed.

These are the facts. This is reality. There is no "equal pay for equal work" problem in America.

FACT #3:

From 2011-2015, men accounted for 92.5% of workplace fatalities.

There are two possible explanations for this stat:

1. Men are inherently clumsy and more likely to step on a rake at work.

Or

2. Women don't bear the same dangerous responsibilities in the workplace.

You will hear the left talk about how there are not enough female CEO's and not enough female engineers. They only talk about the lucrative jobs. If we are talking about a fair and equal society when it comes to the top 100 companies having "x" number of female CEOs, we also need to talk about every other job across the board. Males and females need to bear the same types of responsibilities when it comes to job positions. Not just the high profile CEO jobs that take up an incredibly small percentage of American jobs, but also the low- and mid-level positions.

This stat is extreme inequality at its definition. Why don't liberals ever address such inequalities? Because doing so goes against their divisive narrative. We will see this theme a lot as these facts come up throughout the book.

FACT #4:

Men are sentenced to 63% more prison time than women for the exact same crime.

This fact is straight out of the far left news site, The Huffington Post. It's ironic that they report such a shocking statistic and still perpetuate the lie of female victimhood in the United States.

This is actual inequality in hard statistics. Yet, I've never heard it talked about by anyone of importance in the media or in our government because it shatters their identity politics strategy that targets women and their vote.

I'm not saying men should feel like victims and take to the streets with baby blue hats made into the male genitalia (pink pussy hat reference), but I am saying that if the left is going to run their entire campaign on equality and fairness, they need to fight for equality and fairness across the board. Not just the demographics that they think are going to garner them the most votes.

FACT #5:

Nearly 4 out of 5 suicides are men.

Are men naturally more depressed? Is there a societal effect causing this? Why doesn't the left ever talk about this?

With almost 45,000 suicides a year in the US that cost our country $69 billion, you'd think this would be a major issue that is talked about all the time in our liberal media. Specifically, because this issue is preventable. That being said, the media and our universities drive home the narratives of the "evil patriarchy" and "toxic masculinity." Is suicide not a campaignable issue because they affect men more than women?

Clearly, this doesn't cause enough outrage for the left to push it. No emotional outrage, no point in pushing it because the people's vote is less easy to sway, right?

FACT #6:

Prostate cancer has a 17.9% mortality rate, breast cancer has a 15.4% mortality rate.

I think this fact is important to include for many reasons. Approximately 266,000 women will be diagnosed with breast cancer in 2018, and around 41,000 will die. About 165,000 men will be diagnosed with prostate cancer in 2018, and around 29,000 will die. Just by looking at the volume of cases, breast cancer is the bigger issue, but they are both significant issues that deserve attention.

Institutions like the NFL do a great thing by promoting research for breast cancer, but do you think that maybe by saying "hey mom, we care about you and your health and will go as far as wearing pink on the football field to prove it" they are gaining mom's approval? Maybe a few ticket sales even? My proof is in the pudding. Why not decide to "create awareness" for lung cancer? After all, in 2018 nearly 154,000 people will die from lung cancer versus the 70,000 that will die of breast and prostate cancer combined.

Breast cancer, lung cancer, prostate cancer ... it's all cancer. Cancer is cancer. Why put a body part to it? Why not promote "cancer awareness" instead? Because of marketing 101: breasts sell tickets. Please take this into consideration when you see companies exploiting this.

The point of this statistic: while the left preaches equality for all, where are they on the issue that strikes men nearly as much as breast cancer strikes women?

FACTS #7 & 8:

1 in 3 women and 1 in 4 men have been victims of physical violence by an intimate partner within their lifetime.

There are over 2,000 domestic violence shelters exclusively for women (most turn away men) and only 2 (TWO) exclusively for men.

This is a stat that you will never see in the mainstream media. The liberal narrative victimizes women and, again, pits them against men in an attempt to capture a vote. This entire first chapter of the book is focused on debunking the narrative of female victimhood, and to me, this one was the most surprising and effective facts in doing that.

When I was in the military, we had quarterly training (just for men) on not abusing or sexually assaulting women. It was made out to be such an epidemic that I honestly felt bad for women. I was an ignorant casualty to the false narratives out there eating what was spoon fed to me. Contrary to the mainstream narrative on women and abuse, this fact (backed by police reports) proves that abuse in relationships affects both men and women and men aren't the toxic-masculine cancers that modern feminists on the left say we are.

Not to mention, where's the equality in the lack of resources for men compared to women in fact #8?

FACT #9:

There is no written rule against women playing in the NFL.

Men and women are biologically different. Men have thicker bone density, higher testosterone, and more muscle mass — things that help them physically excel past their female counterparts. Why is that a bad thing? We each have different strengths and instead of abandoning those strengths in the name of absolute equality, let's recognize those differences that we have and celebrate them.

In the modern feminist's mind, we should all put our daughters in pads, hurl footballs at them until they're fully grown at 5'3" 126 pounds, and hope they make it into the league. Sorry girls, we're not all equal in every aspect of life, and this is one of them. It's not a bad thing.

Unfortunately, we all can't be anything we want to be like some kids are taught growing up because if we let our 5'3" daughters line up across from Brian Urlacher they might die.

Men and women are physically different. It's a reality of our being, and that's okay.

FACT #10:

34% of college students are men.

We have affirmative action policies. We have women's rights groups on campus, black student unions, Hispanic student unions, Asian student unions, gay rights, trans rights ... Liberals have created a group for every possible demographic out there in the name of equality and representation.

What are they missing about equality in this situation? 66% versus 34%? Doesn't seem very equal and representative to me. I'll repeat it a thousand times: the left does not care about true "equality." They want your vote.

FACT #11:

There has been a 59% decline in total sperm count in men over the last 4 decades.

The possible reasons for this decrease are endless: Cell phones, computers, video games, increased sexual activity because of social acceptance of such behavior, more work, and less sleep. We don't know the exact cause of this decline, it is likely a combination of all of these societal changes, but it should be cause for alarm for any society, and we should ask why this is happening and try and find out.

"Toxic masculinity is society's problem, screw men. Their issues aren't actual issues." I have heard these words before. Several times.

Equality for all, though.

FACT #12:

From 2000 to 2014, of all people who received inpatient care who identified as transgender, only 4,118 underwent transgender surgery.

For the sake of this argument, I'm going to use the US population in 2014 to represent this 15-year span. The population that year was 318.6 million people.

Before I tell you the massive percentage of the US that underwent transgender surgery during that time, I want you to think about how much on-air news coverage is spent debating the transgender issue. The left has made it a cornerstone of their platform.

Is it an issue that deserves so much attention?

If you consider .00129% of the population deserving of massive chunks of our time spent debating, then yes. But I would beg to differ. In my opinion, the hundreds of thousands of people who are going to die from cancer every year deserve more attention.

I am of the libertarian mindset on the transgender issue. Liberty allows you to do whatever you want unless you are harming someone else. Want to chop off your manhood? Well, I guess if that's your thing and you think it'll make you happy then go right ahead. I'm not going to waste my time telling you that you can't because I believe there are more significant issues in our society.

FACTS #13 & 14:

Hillary Clinton said, "I think a marriage is as a marriage has always been, between a man and a woman."

Barack Obama said, "I believe marriage is between a man and a woman. I am not in favor of gay marriage."

These quotes are very confusing when you stop to think about how these two led the Democratic party that claims they are the party campaigning for gay rights. It is one of MANY examples of how the left tries to utilize identity politics to their favor. Who cares what Hillary and Barack actually think about an issue, right? They changed their ideas about gay rights because they felt it was the best way to gain more votes. This flip-flopping on the issues is the problem and why I included these quotes as facts.

The left as we know it has become the face of the gay community, but how the hell did the gay community fall for it?

Again, my solution is of the libertarian ideology. Do you like to sleep with people of the same sex? Whatever, it doesn't affect me or anyone else but you and your partner so I don't care. Liberty allows you to do whatever you want. Gay marriage? "Separation of church and state." Marriage is a religious ceremony, but how did the state get involved in a religious affair in the first place? It no longer is separated, the state is involved, and gay marriage will be around forever, whether the left tries to convince you that the right wants to take it away or not. Don't listen to them.

FACT #15:

Trump has appointed the first-ever female CIA Director, the first-ever black female Marine General, and had the first-ever woman campaign director to win a presidential campaign.

Google these accomplishments for women, and you will find them highly underreported. For a campaign that ran on "shattering the glass ceiling," they didn't care too much about shattering these glass ceilings.

The women above are now some of the most powerful people that have ever lived. And to undermine their achievement just because you're mad that you lost an election or because you don't like President Trump is shameful. This response is what children do when they don't get to have chicken nuggets for dinner instead of pork chops and broccoli. Give these women the respect you demanded we show to Hillary — they deserve it.

Might I add, thank you, President Donald Trump, for finding the best possible candidates for the job which happened to be these Americans.

IN CONCLUSION

If I didn't drive it home enough, these facts on gender were to prove that equality does not matter to the left, because 1) they only fight for equality of the demographics they see as easily manipulated with their emotion-based tactics and 2) when they actually get equality and progress it is not recognized.

I said it before, but I want to reiterate that the stats already presented in this book that are lopsided against men are not my battle cry for men to stand up and fight for equality. The main point that I hope these stats helped prove is this; if liberals are going to preach equality and progression, they need to preach it for all on every single issue, not just the problems that fit their narrative and target demographics.

Also, be sure to research your party's platform and slogans. You may find out the "70¢ on the dollar" is big pile of Democrat lies.

ON GUNS, CRIME AND POLICE

I will never forget when I went to buy my first handgun. I walked into Gander Mountain, up to the counter and said, "Hey sir, I'd like to buy this 9mm Smith and Wesson."

"Alright which one, exactly?" He asked.

"This one right here," I said pointing at the gun I wanted to buy.

"Great, let me get it out for you so you can see. I'm also going to need your license and your permit so I can get the paperwork started."

"Permit?" I said like a fool.

"Uh, yea, your permit."

"I mean, I'm signed up for a class next weekend, that's why I'm here so I can buy a gun to have for the class."

The man smirked. It was clear he'd been in this situation hundreds of times before. He went on to explain that you need a permit to buy a handgun and until I took the class, went through a background check and officially got my permit, I couldn't buy a gun.

I was shocked. The liberal media and all my uninformed liberal friends said that I could literally walk into the store and buy whatever gun I wanted!

It is far from the truth, and laws do vary by state, but the liberal media still pushes this false idea. There are MANY common sense gun laws in place, today. No gun owner that I know says there shouldn't be any gun laws, because that's insane. I don't want anyone with a violent criminal history buying a gun, do you? The great thing is that they can't. The left won't tell you that though.

To finish my gun purchasing story:

I took a class with one of my best buddies on a Saturday. We each spent $70 to take the 6-hour class, 5 hours in the classroom and an hour on the shooting range. After that, we took our certificates to the Sheriff's Office where we paid more money to have them run background checks on us. We received our gun licenses in the mail a few weeks later and went back to Gander Mountain.

"Got all your paperwork?" The same man asked with a shit eating grin.

"Got it!" I said, "I'll take that one!"

"Alright, let's see your driver's license and your permit, I'll start your background check."

"Background check? I just did that with the sheriff's office?"

"Yea, it's another one."

I sat there for another hour while he ran my record through the FBI database.

A month's worth of waiting, hundreds of dollars of training, certificates, and two background checks, and I finally had a gun.

Reality doesn't quite compare with the liberal gun narrative, does it?

Here are some shocking gun facts that you may or may not have known. Spread them with care and watch plants of logic and reason bloom.

FACT #16:

The number of guns in America has increased more than 50% since 1993. In that same period of time, the gun homicide rate has dropped by 50%.

Statistics is the practice of gathering large amounts of data, quantifying that data and drawing conclusions based on that data. It is neither liberal or conservative. Numbers are numbers, and they do not lie. Fact #16 is a conundrum for the anti-gun narrative.

What conclusions can we draw from this statistic? We can easily conclude that due to the increased number of guns in our country, there is a correlating decrease in homicides; therefore more guns are preventing more murder. It could be that the citizens of our country are better defended and that evil people are more fearful of those people defending themselves.

It is also reasonable to conclude that guns are not responsible for murders when they do happen and that the majority of people who own guns are responsible owners. The motives of the person who decides to pull the trigger should be taken into account. If guns were responsible for killings, we would very likely see the number of homicides increase as the number of guns increase.

FACTS #17 & 18:

National average police response time is 11 minutes.

It takes 1 second for a bad person to harm you.

There are two main reasons to arm yourself — for hunting and self-defense. If somebody approaches you with ill intentions, it is only reasonable to want to defend yourself.

If somebody tries to rob you or hurt you, they are very likely going to do so while being armed. If you find yourself up against an armed criminal and you are unarmed, you are at a huge disadvantage right off the bat. The other disadvantage is that you probably aren't expecting something like that to happen on any given day. Unfortunately, wherever you are in the world, being attacked is a real possibility. The great thing about our country is that we allow you to give yourself the upper hand.

Let's pretend for a moment that the left had their way and we didn't have guns.

A man twice your size approaches you with a gun and tells you to give him your wallet. Without a gun on you or deadly MMA skills, what do you do? Under the left's logic, you should hope that the attacker allows you to call a timeout, pull out your phone to dial 9-1-1 and then wait 11 minutes for the police to arrive so THEY can defend you.

I promise that isn't going to happen. What will happen is that in about 10 seconds you will either willingly hand over your wallet and lose some essential possessions to a bad person while maybe getting hurt before he leaves you alone, or that man will force you to give him your wallet, and you will get hurt.

It happens every day in every country and should be enough reason for anyone to want to own a gun and defend themselves. Take your well-being into your own hands or be the one willing to step up for those who aren't willing to handle a gun.

FACT #19:

Deaths by gun types in 2016:

Handguns = 7,105

Rifles = 374

Shotguns = 262

When the liberal mainstream media tries to push "common sense" gun control laws, what do they usually target? They target AR-15's which are rifles. Looking at the hard objective data, if you're targeting guns is it very common sense to target a gun that accounts for roughly 5% the amount of murders committed by handguns? Not to mention that 5% is assuming that ALL of those 374 rifle murders are committed by AR-15's. The answer is no, it's not common sense. So, why does the left push this narrative when it is clearly misguided?

FACT #20:

Knives kill 4 times as many people a year in the US as all rifles combined.

In 2016, 1,604 people were murdered with knives. That's more than four times as many as all people murdered with rifles. Where are the protests over knife murders? The argument goes "if there are no guns, there are no gun murders." It is such a lazy argument. We can say the same about everything that is considered bad:

"If there are no knives, there are no knife murders."

"If there are no drugs, there are no drug deaths."

"If there are no cars, there are no drunk driving deaths."

Walk away from this horrible argument. The stats do not support the outrage. Don't let the left skew your reason and get your vote.

FACT #21:

The "AR" in AR-15 stands for ArmaLite Rifle, not "assault rifle."

ArmaLite is a manufacturer's brand name. They manufacture rifles much like Kleenex is a brand name for a company that manufactures tissues.. We had to include this fact because of the misinformation out there spread by people who don't even own or shoot guns. In my personal life I've heard uninformed people talking about the "AR" in "AR-15" standing for "assault rifle." Sorry to burst your bubble.

FACT #22:

80% of all gun homicides are gang related. Gang related homicides accounted for 8,900 gun-related deaths in 2010 and 11,100 in 2011.

As we dissect the left's gun narrative, it unravels in a hurry. Four out of five gun murders are gang related. To me, that says the numbers relating to gun violence in America are not actually a gun problem, especially if a tiny fraction of the country is in a gang, and they account for a majority of the gun murders.

We have a gang problem, not a gun problem. Plain and simple.

FACT #23:

In 2013, Obama's CDC estimated that 300,000-5 million lives were saved by defensive gun use annually.

Quote from the article:

"Almost all national survey estimates indicate that defensive gun uses by victims are at least as common as offensive uses by criminals, with estimates of annual uses ranging from about 500,000 to more than 3 million…"

The left pushes for more gun control whenever they can, but with numbers like these (coming from a government source under Obama) how can anyone reasonably think that makes sense? I wonder how many more people would be murdered each year if millions of people weren't able to defend themselves.

FACT #24:

Gun silencers do not silence. They reduce noise just enough to not destroy your eardrum.

On October 2nd, 2017 right after the Las Vegas Massacre, Hillary Clinton tweeted:

"The crowd (in Las Vegas) fled at the sound of gunshots. Imagine the deaths if the shooter had a silencer."

This is the perfect example of leftist leadership getting an emotional rise out of people to push their agenda in a time of vulnerability. What Hillary Clinton tweeted is complete and utter propaganda and is shameful. Americans have a sensationalized idea of gun silencers in their minds because of Hollywood movies, and she exploited that at the perfect time.

Gun silencers do not silence a gun. Gun silencers are designed to help people who shoot frequently to save their hearing; the noise is still very loud. A silencer would not have made the Vegas shooter invisible and would not have made the event any more tragic than it already was.

Also, in case you were wondering, you can't just walk into a store and buy a silencer. You have to: be a resident of the 42 states that allow silencers to be purchased, must be a US resident, must be legally eligible to purchase a firearm (refer to my story at the beginning of this chapter), must pass a BATFE background check, must be 21 to purchase from a dealer, and 18 to purchase from another citizen.

FACT #25:

A gun cannot fire itself.

Newton's first law of motion states that an object in motion will stay in motion, or an object at rest will stay at rest unless acted upon by an outside force.

A gun is an object, and these laws apply to it. Science is the mantra to many in the mainstream media when it comes to agendas like global warming, but science is ignored when it comes to very basic things like fact #25.

It is a bit nauseating to know that this fact has to be included on this list, but it is a fact that is too often ignored. With every other crime, the person is blamed:

A drunk driver is blamed for the death. THEY caused an accident, not the alcohol or vehicle.

A bomber is blamed for mass casualties. THEY caused the explosion, not the bomb.

Cane is responsible for murdering Abel, not the stone.

Why is there a different standard when it comes to guns? Why is someone's mental stability not the reason for the gun crime? Why is the reason for the crime not attributed to an evil ideology in this person's head? These questions and science are always ignored by the mainstream media and leftist politicians because rationality and logic don't get people charged up. The easiest thing to do is to blame an inanimate object and call for "change," because why? You guessed it. It's a great vote grabber.

FACT #26:

262 million people were murdered by their governments in the 20th Century.

A common argument against our second amendment is that it's outdated and we have no need for it in today's society. The facts beg to differ. We have example after example throughout other countries in the world that show exactly why we still need the second amendment. Power corrupts, people are corruptible, and history proves that. We cannot ignore history, and we especially cannot ignore what is happening around us in other countries at this very moment.

262 million people. This number is staggering. One also has to realize that the 20th century was not that long ago. For you timekeepers out there it was less than 18 years ago, and since humans have not evolved or been divinely changed in that short period, we can expect governments to continue to kill people. Which is why you will see us, for the remainder of our lives, continue to uphold our constitution and the 2nd amendment. An armed citizenry is the last line of defense against tyranny.

FACT #27:

An estimated 10,000 unarmed Chinese Nationals were murdered in Tiananmen Square by their own government in 1989.

This is one of the worst massacres committed by a government on its own citizens in recent history. The exact number of deaths is unknown because why would a corrupt government release the real number? For all we know, it could be much higher, but the two main points remain: 1) this was very recent and 2) these poor people protesting for liberty were unarmed, and they were slaughtered like fish in a barrel.

What would have happened in the US?

If the US government began firing upon its own citizens, members of the crowd would have fired back and very likely have saved some lives. Not only that, 100 million plus gun owners in our country would be activated and would have the duty to take action against the heinous crime being committed. Unfortunately, people in China didn't get the justice they deserved. They would have in America, I promise you that.

FACT #28:

Venezuela banned private gun ownership in 2012; now, in 2018 Venezuela has the 3rd highest murder rate in the world.

In 2012, socialist Venezuela passed a bill with the intention to "disarm all citizens." The result? The world's 3rd highest murder rate. How can that be? How can people still be murdered if they don't have guns to murder each other with? Would the murder rate be as high if citizens had guns to defend themselves with against criminals?

For every 100,000 people in Venezuela, about 57 people are murdered. In comparison, the overall US homicide rate in 2015 was 4.9, and the gun homicide rate was 3.03. If guns kill, it would be logical to say that the US would have the highest rate in the world considering we own nearly half the world's population of guns. This is not the case, but "guns kill" is the false narrative that is pushed. Venezuela proves that banning guns does not prevent murder, and also gives strength to the argument that guns are needed for self-defense

FACTS #29 & 30:

Honduras has the highest homicide rate in the world, ranks 88th in gun ownership.

Switzerland has one of the lowest homicide rates in the world, ranks 3rd in gun ownership.

HONDURAS & SWITZERLAND BOTH HAVE POPULATIONS OF JUST OVER 8 MILLION PEOPLE.

We wanted to include these facts because you may have seen a viral post going around about the comparison of Honduras and Switzerland. The post claimed that Honduras had the highest murder rate in the world and the Honduras government banned guns and that Switzerland had the lowest murder rate in the world and it is mandatory to own guns there. This is false, but it's pretty damn close to the truth.

I'm not defending the inaccuracies of the viral meme. Whoever made it should have been more precise. I'm just saying that these claims are worth looking into and when you do look into it there is some valuable information. When "debunking" this claim "fact checkers" like Politifact and Snopes actually contradict the left's gun argument.

While debunking this meme (refer to the source cited for this fact) Politifact essentially says that these two countries are not comparable due to factors like poverty, lifestyles, laws, etc. But wait a minute. So, guns *are* inanimate objects, and other factors *do* matter? What happened to the "guns kill people so let's ban them" argument?

I hope seeing how the left flip-flops in their narrative is making it easier for you to walk away, and we are just at the tip of the iceberg.

FACT #31:

London's murder rate soared 44%, and incidents involving firearms increased 11% in 2017.

According to the BBC, "The UK has some of the toughest gun control laws in the world. If you want to own a gun, it is very difficult to do so."

Wouldn't you think that murder would stay low with some of the toughest gun control laws in the world? Wouldn't you think incidents involving firearms would be virtually zero with the toughest gun control laws in the world?

This fact further proves that evil people will find a way to kill, regardless of what a piece of paper written by the lawmakers of a country says. Let me just remind you that this is a highly developed Western country in which these murder rates are soaring. How is this happening? Could it be the incredible amount of immigrants that don't believe in Western civilization? I'm not saying it is, I'm just asking questions here. Until these questions are answered the problem will continue, and some of the strictest gun laws in the world will not prevent it.

ON MASS SHOOTINGS

FACT #32:

Annual death rates from mass shootings per MILLION people from 2009-2015:

Norway	1.888
Serbia	0.381
France	0.347
Macedonia	0.337
Albania	0.206
Slovakia	0.185
Switzerland	0.142
Finland	0.132
Belgium	0.128
Czech Republic	0.123
UNITED STATES	0.089

Mass shootings are always an unfortunate tragedy, and they should concern us, but politicians that use them to push their anti-gun agendas based on false and skewed information should concern us even more.

It's sad, but the media and liberal politicians jump at the bit to push for gun control when these horrific events happen. They waste virtually no time, almost like they are ready and waiting for them to happen so they can do so.

Is America the most likely place you will die from a mass shooting? That answer is no. Less than a one in a million chance you will die in a mass shooting. You have a better chance of getting struck by lighting *this year*. We will continue to hit this point on the head, they push this because these are tragic events in which people get emotional, and when people get emotional, it's easier to get them to think a certain way. Shame on the mainstream media and shame on the leftist politicians for manipulating people. We need to figure out why people decide to commit mass shootings, but I can tell you right now that it's not because of guns.

FACT #33:

No NRA member has ever committed a mass shooting.

We've all heard it in the news, in social media, and from misinformed people in our lives:

"The murderous NRA!"

"The NRA is a terrorist organization!"

"Blame the NRA for the school shooting!"

These are some of the most common phrases thrown around in the news and by leftist talking heads. These statements are clearly not true and should be cause for many to walk away.

The NRA promotes responsible gun ownership while protecting our constitution. That being said, the liberal leadership in our White House and in our media need to point the finger at someone, and what better group to blame than the largest gun owning group of Americans who are also their political enemies?

It's political science 101. "Mud Slinging." Who can paint their opponent in a darker light? The sad part is people actually buy into it.

FACT #34:

The worst school massacres in the history of mankind (all using firearms):

1. 2004-Russia 334 dead
2. 2000-Indonesia 191 dead
3. 1990-Sri Lanka 158 dead
4. 2014-Pakistan 149 dead
5. 2015-Kenya 148 dead
6. 2001-Kenya 67 dead

What we hear all the time is that school shootings are strictly a problem in the US "because of how many guns are in the US, because of the 2nd amendment and because of the *gun culture*." Or at least that's what the left preaches.

Clearly, this is not just a US problem. The fact above actually indicates that it is a *bigger* problem in other countries.

FACT #35:

75% of mass shooters use a handgun to carry out their shootings.

    This fact brings us back to fact #19 and further questions, why and how can liberals push the "ban rifles" narrative when rifles aren't even the tools being used most often in shootings?

    According to the objective realities of the world, their narrative is way off. That being said, it's easier to push the anti-gun narrative against a gun that looks scary versus a gun that people see in movies and on the hips of police officers every day. Subconsciously we are conditioned to be comfortable around handguns, but when people see a gun that looks like it could be shot in war? Bingo, the left has a ticket into the emotion bin of irrational thinkers.

FACT #36:

97.8% of mass public shootings have occurred in "Gun-Free Zones" since 1950.

Laws do not prevent bad people from doing bad things. How much more evidence is needed to prove this?

Most campuses and many business establishments put "no gun" signs on their front doors. Do you really think that an evil person with evil intentions is even going to stop and read a sign?

Furthermore, do you think if Congress made it punishable by death to carry guns in a gun-free zone that it would stop this person? The answer is no and stats like this prove that, but are conveniently ignored by the left.

FACT #37:

Out of the 27 worst mass shootings in US history, 26 of the shooters were raised without their biological fathers.

Fathers play a vital role in a child's life. Without a father, kids have higher chances of poverty, as well as trouble with the law. Is it a lack of discipline, love, and guidance? Is it a built up anger at the biological father? Whatever the case may be, you will see more statistics shortly that show how important fatherhood is in a child's life.

ON CRIME AND POVERTY

FACTS #38, 39 & 40:

Children in fatherless homes are 4 times as likely to be poor.

A child raised in a single parent household is 5 times as likely to grow up in poverty versus a child raised by married parents.

Children in single-parent homes are twice as likely to kill themselves.

Two parents bringing in two incomes are better than one. More money equals more opportunity because of the increased amount of resources available to them.

Two parents disciplining is better than one. Also, when considering the biological differences between men and women, men are bigger, have deeper voices, and are more intimidating to children than the women who nurse our children and have a different bond.

Two parents equal double the amount of time a child gets with an adult. This may not always be true in every household, but one parent has 24 hours in their day. Two parents equal 48 hours in the day combined. My

Minnesotan public school math education tells me that's DOUBLE the chances a child gets to spend with a parent.

Why are single-parent households so common in our country?

If you have not researched Lyndon B Johnson's "War on Poverty," you must. It explains how his policies incentivized single-parent households with welfare. It explains why single-parent households have tripled since his policies went into effect. For what it's worth, he was a Democrat.

FACTS #41, 42 & 43:

Of students in grades 1 through 12, 39% (17.7 million) live in homes absent their biological fathers.

57.6% of black children, 31.2% of Hispanic children, and 20.7% of white children are living absent their biological father.

72% of black children are born out of wedlock.

    All of these children, no matter their ethnicity, have a higher chance of living a life of poverty, crime, and mental illness. It is not a skin color issue, but a cultural issue and an acceptance of norms in each community. By looking at the numbers, it is clear that the number of fatherless homes in the black community is higher than that of Hispanics and whites. Many on the left would argue that it's because of the war on drugs incarcerating millions of black fathers. Dylan and I both agree that the war on drugs is a lost cause and must end. But, to say that every black man is in prison for non-violent offenses is far from the truth, yet that is the narrative of the left, and it further perpetuates the victimhood mentality. There is no accountability at an individual level with the left's narrative, and that is one of the problems. The left has pandered to the black community by victimizing the entire group, and it enables things like the cultural norms you see in the facts above.

Statistics tell us that fatherless homes are one of the roots of many lifelong problems for individuals. The acceptance of the fatherless norm in the black community is alarmingly evident in the most objective crime state there is, murder.

FACTS #44 & 45:

Over 50% of US murders are committed by black males (6% of the population).

90% of murdered blacks are killed by other blacks.

The numbers in these facts are a result of fatherless homes, not because a person has a darker pigment in their skin. It is a bigger problem in the black community because they have been targeted by the left for decades.

We wanted to include this murder statistic because it debunks many of the left's talking points. You will very often hear the left say that black men are wrongfully incarcerated and don't commit more crime. Well, if there is a dead body, there's absolutely no refuting that a crime took place. Someone did it, and 50% of the time it was by someone who very likely didn't grow up with a father. Same with mass murderers (who happened to be a majority of white males).

If you don't grow up with your dad, you will very likely lead a life of crime and despair.

Again, we attribute this to Lyndon B Johnson's War on Poverty that targeted people in the black community.

FACT #46:

In 2012, blacks committed 560,600 acts of violence against whites, whites committed 99,403 acts of violence against blacks.

More debunking of the left's narrative. As I write this, Anne Hathaway said that "ALL black people fear for their lives daily." Do the hard facts and objective realities of the world support her claim? Should black people fear for their lives daily?

Nope. Not even close.

85% of interracial crime is black on white. Those numbers are even more staggering when considering the population component of this equation. When we see movement's like Black Lives Matter that are being pushed in the media, we are told that anyone with white skin is the problem. When you also have a group named "Black Lives Matter," you are insinuating that swaths of people think that black lives don't matter. It's not only absurd to say such things, but it's extremely divisive. Interracial crime is incited by the media and race pimps like Al Sharpton telling their followers to get angry (and vote Democrat). When they tell their followers to get angry, violence happens, and nothing is solved.

Imagine being at work and telling your fellow employees to "get angry" while offering no solution to the "injustice." Will the company run very well?

But hey, back to Identity Politics 101: when you point a finger, you create a common enemy among a group of people, which in turns makes it very easy to capture 12% of the American vote with the black community.

ON IDENTITY POLITICS

FACT #47:

A total of 21 Democrats opposed the Civil Rights Act in 1964, only 1 of them ever became a Republican.

But ... wasn't there a "Big Switch?"

I hate to break it to you, but the "Big Switch" was a big fat lie to distance the left from their dark past. Can you imagine every single Republican and Democrat today suddenly changing their entire belief system and switching parties, or adopting the other party's belief system? That doesn't happen unless you're on an acid trip, or unless you are Hillary Clinton switching up her platform every few years.

Why do people believe the Big Switch happened then?

Because that is what we are taught to think at an early age.

Like many of you, I remember sitting in my high school history teacher's class (yes, she was incredibly liberal) learning about the big switch. At 16 all I cared about was football and girls, I didn't think twice about what they were teaching me. Most 16-year-olds are in the same position. Why would an authoritative figure (in this case a teacher) teach me a bunch of bologna?

Let me be clear, I think this teacher, who was a nice person, taught this stuff to us full heartedly believing it herself. As do most. The question then comes, where did she learn this stuff?

Our Liberal colleges.

FACT #48:

Robert Byrd, the longest-serving member in congressional history (56 years, 320 days), was an Exalted Cyclops in the KKK. He was also a lifelong Democrat until he died in 2010.

Mr. Robert Byrd didn't get the message about the big switch as he was a lifelong Democrat until the day he died in 2010. He is also the longest-serving member of Congress ever, who also happened to be a leader in the KKK.

A nice, little inconvenient truth for liberals.

Hillary also called him a mentor. She also has a photo of them kissing each other's cheeks!

Think for yourself, stop believing everything the left spouts out.

FACT #49:

The KKK donated $20,000 to Hillary's campaign in 2016.

"For the KKK, Clinton is our choice," said Will Quigg, California Grand Dragon for the Loyal White Knights.

Isn't it funny how the script was flipped in the media right after this came out? They were quick to report that David Duke supports Trump. The media ran this in the headlines for weeks and not the fact that Hillary received money from the KKK. Nice diversion by the mainstream media, huh?

FACT #50:

Every Grand Wizard of the KKK was a Democrat, even David Duke at one point.

One of many inconvenient truths for the Democratic party. If you remember in the 2016 election, David Duke came out in favor of Trump and the media ran with it. "Trump loves the KKK!" And here we are today with that narrative that is repeatedly spewed. The sad thing is that there is truth behind the saying "repeat something often enough and it becomes truth." It's called brainwashing, and the Rachel Maddows and Don Lemons of the world have repeated this lie so much that they have gotten their viewers to believe their lies. And to their brainwashed viewers, it is the truth, which is sad because objective facts beg to differ.

FACT #51:

The KKK boasts a membership of an estimated 5,000-8,000 members in the US today. Translation: .002% of the population.

Everyone who voted for Trump is a Nazi or a KKK member though! Painting people as a racist when they aren't is the cheapest form of political mudslinging. History and facts are easily used to prove these claims otherwise. It is truly sad to see people believe them.

FACTS #52, 53, 54 & 55:

The 13th Amendment (abolishment of slavery) passed with 100% Republican Support and 23% Democrat support.

The 14th Amendment (gave citizenship to freed slaves) had 94% Republican support and 0% Democrat support.

The 15th Amendment (gave freed black men the right to vote) had 100% Republican support and 0% Democrat support.

80% of Republicans supported the Civil Rights Act of 1964, only 63% of Democrats Supported it.

    If I were a Democrat, I would run from my past as well by touting the Big Switch. I don't blame them. They have an incredibly horrible record when it comes to equal rights. Back in the time of the 13th, 14th and 15th amendments, the Democrats owned most of the country's slaves and were profiting hugely off them. Freeing black people, making them citizens and giving them the right to vote would cause them tremendous losses in the bank. Not only that, If I were a slave and had just been given the right to vote, I sure as heck wouldn't be voting for the people who made me bust my butt picking cotton all day for nothing in return but some food and a crappy bed.

How then did Democrats trick the black community into voting for them in our modern society? Again, we come back to Lyndon B Johnson's war on poverty. The boom in welfare. Think about it, if you are poor and someone comes along and says, "hey, you're poor AND a victim, here's a check. Also, that Republican over there wants to make you work for this check. Us Democrats? Nope, we'll just give it to you." I would probably take the free money, and keep that person in power by voting for them so I could continue to get that money! Why wouldn't you? That's money you can use to support your kids and get them through school. The problem with welfare is that it isn't enough to support your family. It's just enough to keep your head above water, but not enough to get out from under the grips of dependence and into success.

Your vote is a politician's and political party's ticket to power. Hundreds of years ago all they had to do was kill someone off to rise to power. Now, they need to trick millions of people, and it's a lot easier than it sounds, case in point, the war on poverty.

FACTS #56 & 57:

The first black Republican Senator was elected in 1870 — Hiram Rhodes Revels.

The first black Democratic Senator was elected in 1992 — Carol Moseley Braun.

It's hard to explain this one if you are a Democrat. Their mythological Big Switch happened decades before they decided it was time to try and run from their past and start electing Black Americans to office. You won't find these people in your high school history books because if they were in there, it might be hard to trick people into buying into the Big Switch.

FACT #58:

Asian Americans would make up 43% of Harvard if academics were the only factor. Because of quotas on demographics, they only make up 19%.

There are no racist laws in this country except for affirmative action laws. Because of quotas and believing that one race is disadvantaged over the other (the definition of racism), liberals are not allowing the best candidates for positions to take those positions. Case in point: Harvard is discriminating against Asian Americans. According to this fact, 24% of positions at Harvard were filled with people that scored lower on their tests. Isn't academia built off of test scores? Aren't test scores supposed to dictate who is smarter? If you are running a business, don't you want the most knowledgeable person in a position so your business will thrive and make more money?

Not to mention, If you were afforded a position due to affirmative action policies, would you genuinely feel accomplished as a person knowing that you got to where you are because of how you looked, and that someone out there was better qualified, but because people in Washington DC patronized you and felt bad for you, you got it instead?

I'd feel a little shameful and even a little guilty.

ON ABORTION

One of the biggest hypocrisies of the left is that they preach equality and opportunity for every single man, woman, and child, yet they don't give an opportunity to hundreds of thousands of babies each year.

Pretend for a minute that you believe abortion is not murder. *If* an abortion does not occur will a baby be born? In case you are stumbling, that answer is yes. Let's rephrase this whole "abortion is murder" thing then and start saying that abortion is "life prevention." The left wants to prevent life from occurring, which is despicable. They are taking an opportunity away from a future person that could very well be the one who changes this world in a very positive way.

Whether you agree or not, the left uses abortion as a political vote machine, and they skew the narrative in a number of ways to get people to think the way *they want* them to think.

FACT #59:

13% of Planned Parenthood patients get abortions, NOT 3%.

Planned Parenthood performed 323,999 abortions in 2014. They saw 2.5 million patients.

Elizabeth Warren and Planned Parenthood supporters claim that only 3% of patients get abortions. Let's do the math on that and see:

323,999/2,500,000=12.95%

Math does not lie. Where's the disconnect here?

They skew their numbers by instead dividing abortions by the number of services *performed*, and not by the number of *patients*. One patient could receive two, four, even ten different services during an appointment. That adds up to 9.4 million services in 2014, instead of 2.5 million, and this is how they skew their numbers. "13% of patients getting abortions" is not the best PR Planned Parenthood and the left want. The worst part about all of this to me is that this information is publicly documented in their annual reports and people still find a way to ignore facts like this.

FACT #60:

Planned Parenthood only makes one adoption referral per 160 abortions performed.

Sad. To enable the "flush your responsibilities" card (abortion) you have to have a complete lack of regard for humans, i.e., Planned Parenthood. It's ironic since regressives (liberals) constantly preach that the Conservatives don't value human life. I'm happy that Planned Parenthood refers one kid but extremely sad that those 160 don't even get a chance.

FACT #61:

Planned Parenthood performs 0.97% of the nation's PAP smears, 1.8% of breast exams, and 30.6% of the nation's abortions.

Hold on a second. You mean to tell me that the 3% thing Elizabeth Warren talks about is an even bigger load of bull?

It is.

We now know that 13% of Planned Parenthood patients get abortions, but that 13% is even more staggering when considering that Planned Parenthood performs nearly 30.6% of the country's abortions.

In the business world, we call that a dominant market presence.

FACT #62:

More black babies are aborted than born in New York City.

Maybe abortion is a little bit racist? I'll repeat it again since it is so important. The lack of opportunity given to all of these babies is dumbfounding and very sad.

FACT #63:

Since Sandy Hook, 138 kids have died in school shootings. In that same time, nearly 4,000,000 babies have been aborted.

Maybe one of those aborted kids could have been a future president or invented something that changed our lives. The same can be said of the 138 kids that have died since Sandy Hook. The point is, one of the left's main vote-getters is school shootings. Yet, they are pro-life prevention. If you can't see how these talking points conflict, you are are allowing yourself to be taken advantage of and deceived.

ON IMMIGRATION

Liberals on capitol hill have made 2018 they year of the illegal immigrant. It is evident that they have made it their point to push illegal immigration as their main vote grabber in the midterms. Since Trump was elected, they have done everything in their power to paint Conservatives negatively, get Trump out of office and take back Congress in the midterms.

They have tried everything from lies about Russian collusion and a porn star to cries of "racism." The only thing that took root was when they posted pictures of kids in cages from 2014 and blamed Trump and his heartless Conservative following. People were outraged. I even spoke with people on the right who were upset, which took me back for a second. That's when I knew this is the topic they are going to hammer home, and they have.

Here are some facts that will hopefully bring you back to reality.

FACT #64:

As of 2010, there were 2,748 linear miles of highway sound barrier walls built in the US to help with traffic noise.

This is an important stat for several reasons. 1) it proves that building 1,100 miles of walls on the southern border is possible and affordable; 2) it begs the questions, why is it okay to build walls to protect our ears from sound, but not okay to build a wall to protect us from drugs and criminals? (Yes, everyone who crosses the border through a route other than the approved checkpoints is a criminal, hence the word illegal immigrant)

And to anyone who says the wall is unrealistic, that it's too big or that the terrain is too tough to build it on, the Chinese built a wall with their hands and a few chisels before Jesus Christ even walked the earth. Don't tell us it's not possible; that is the laziest argument regarding the wall.

FACT #65:

Hungarian border wall cases of illegal immigration:

3 months pre-wall = 295,831

3 months post-wall = 1,138

Just like gun laws and social norms, and just like societal structures like communism and capitalism, we need to look at history and countries of the present for examples where we can learn. It is that easy. This is an excellent example in the modern day that proves a wall works. Three months before in Hungary and three months after. Do we need to go over these numbers or do they speak for themselves?

FACT #66:

80% of Central American women and girls are raped during their border crossing attempts.

It's ironic seeing this fact come from the Huffington Post. They are a proponent of illegal immigration, and they are a proponent of women and their voice. Just like with women's issues in the Middle East, the left here in the United States cares solely about women in our country. Which makes sense because the women in America are the ones with votes to cast. Why should the left care about issues outside of America? It doesn't push their vote machine.

How hypocritical of the left, especially the Huffington Post, to report on an alarming issue such as fact number 66 and continue to promote illegal immigration. Shame on them.

FACTS #67 & 68:

As much as 94% of heroin comes into the US through Mexico.

Heroin addiction costs the US more than $50 billion per year.

The wall will cost taxpayers a total of about $20 billion to build. In the border situation with heroin we can get that money back. Even if we cut that traffic down by *half* with the wall, theoretically we can save $25 billion on the Heroin problem. Notice what I just said, on ONE SINGLE ISSUE. Illegal immigration costs Americans much more than money. It also costs us as a society by the number of people addicted to heroin.

FACT #69:

Of the 10.8 million legal immigrants since 2008, 7.8 million came through chain migration.

"Donald Trump and his supporters hate immigrants!" That statement is not true. With over a million legal immigrants a year, we are a very welcoming country. And for every person that gets into our country legally, there are dozens more waiting. Wouldn't it be nice to spend the money we would save from illegal immigration to help get more legal immigrants in who do it the right way? Unfortunately, illegals hold the line up and make it unfair for everyone.

Imagine you owned an apartment building with 100 rooms. Each one occupied by someone who works 1 of the 100 jobs in the community to pay for their room. All of a sudden 100 people show up unannounced. Where do they sleep? Is there a job for them to make money? If there's not work for them, those people still need money to get the daily necessities like food. Will they steal to get that money? If they steal will they hurt their victims?

This is a harsh reality that liberals ignore. We can't just open our borders. Emotional thinking looks past the logistics behind open borders. Being a leader means being able to look at the objective facts and make a decision, sometimes a hard one. It would be amazing if we could accept into our lives everyone that asks to come in, but we can't. We have to fix our issues first, and our President thankfully recognizes that.

FACT #70:

1 in 5 federal inmates are foreign born, 90% of those are illegal.

There are so many ways to save our country a lot of money; illegals in our prisons is one. One inmate costs taxpayers almost $32,000 a year. Can you imagine if we were able to cut the number of illegal immigrants in our federal prison system? There are roughly 50,000 illegals in our federal prison system, at $32,000 a year that adds up to $1.6 billion annually. Add it to the source of money saved from the wall.

With how important teaching liberal ideals in colleges is to the left, you'd think that they'd rather give $32,000 a year to students across the country; 50,000 votes is enough to sway a state! But hey, greed gets the best of people, they already know they can get those student's votes, and now they are trying to get the added votes across the border.

FACT #71:

Migrants from Latin America and the Caribbean sent home $69 billion last year.

Why is this such a big issue? For starters, $69 billion is a massive sum of money. Second, basic economics tells us that the more money there is circulating in an economy, the better. Every dollar spent inside the United States keeps our economy going. When items are purchased, the business owner sees their revenue increase while simultaneously putting tax money into the pot. With higher revenues, the business owner can hire more people and create better products. With more tax money we can build better roads, schools, etc. With more jobs, more people will be making more money and buying more things and bringing it full circle back to the business owner. The cycle of a healthy economy continues to snowball.

What if you remove one of those links in the cycle or one link isn't healthy? What if you remove $69 billion from that cycle? That money is not going to be spent here in the United States, it's not going to help American businesses, and if not spent here it will not produce tax money for our country. Calling for higher taxes on remittances (money sent out of the country), does not seem so unreasonable, does it? What if those taxes went to the wall?

FACT #72:

Illegal immigration costs taxpayers $116 billion each year.

The left promotes fairness and equality for all, but how in the world is this fair and equal to every single American that plays by the rules?

To reiterate, liberty allows us to do whatever we want, and I'm on board with that as long as the intentional actions of an individual do not infringe negatively on the lives of other individuals. In this case, costing taxpayers $116 billion is a very adverse action to every American individual who pays taxes. If you worked yesterday and earned money legally, you will pay taxes. That means you dedicated a fraction of your time on the job to illegal immigrants. Time is irreplaceable, money is a social contract that represents our time, and illegal immigrants cost Americans both. Enough is enough.

FACT #73:

For every child at the border separated from their parents, 1,400 American children are separated from their parents due to incarceration.

2.7 million American children have parents who are incarcerated. Compare that to the 2,500 children at the border the left has banded together to virtue signal.

Once again, people not of this country take precedence to the left. Once again, it all comes back to the theme of this book, how can they get more votes?

FACTS #74A & 74B:

51% of immigrants use welfare.

73% of immigrants from Central America/Mexico use welfare.

This stat is fascinating for many reasons and raises many questions and even answers.

The first answer is that this proves America indeed goes out of its way to help immigrants. As we said, over 10 million people have legally immigrated to our country since 2008. According to this, 5 million are on welfare. We are helping them probably more than any other country would.

A question that is brought up is, if we need to help these people so much, are we actually helping them? If they are on welfare that means they are failing to adapt in some form or another. Is our welfare system too easy for immigrants to get? Are we vetting and bringing in productive members into our society? Again, this is not to paint all legal immigrants poorly, but with such an alarming stat as the one in #73, we need to ask these hard questions and figure out solutions.

I am 110% on board for people coming to our country, that's how we grow and create a better society, but we need to make sure the people coming here want to be here and can help our country. We have plenty of problems at home that need to be taken care of before we start trying to take on more things to try and solve, like 5 million more people on welfare.

FACT #75:

In 2017, ICE agents rescued 518 human trafficking victims and 904 children subject to exploitation.

But, from members on the left, you will hear that ICE is a terrorist organization. The only thing they terrorize are votes for Democrats.

FACT #76:

24 million voter registrations (1 in 8) are either invalid or inaccurate and about 2.75 million people are said to be registered to vote in more than one state.

This is coming from Supreme Court Justice Alito. We included this stat under the immigration section of our book because this is why immigration is so important to Democrats and why they campaign for it. It gives many blue states more votes (higher population) and gives them a higher electoral allocation and more US Representative seats. Don't believe me? Jump to #77.

FACT #77:

Undocumented citizens are included in the census and therefore, the electoral distribution.

And here it is, straight off the government website:

"Are undocumented residents (aliens) in the 50 states included in the apportionment population counts?

Yes, all people (citizens and noncitizens) with a usual residence in the 50 states are to be included in the census and thus in the apportionment counts."

Is it all starting to make sense yet on why the left loves illegal immigration?

FACT #78:

Quotes on immigration:

Bill Clinton - "We are a nation of immigrants. But we are also a nation of laws. It is wrong and ultimately self-defeating for a nation of immigrants to permit the kind of abuse of our immigration laws we have seen in recent years, and we must do more to stop it."

Chuck Schumer - "People who enter the US without our permission are illegal aliens."

Obama - "We simply cannot allow people into the U.S. undocumented."

Hillary - "Just because your child gets across the border, that doesn't mean the child gets to stay."

You can't make this stuff up. The "Big Switch" happens on a daily basis with Democrat politicians. One day they believe marriage is between a man and a woman, the next they are marching in gay parades. One day they have their boots on the throat of the border, the next they are welcoming illegal immigrants at the voting booths with open arms.

ON OBAMA

FACT #79:

The Obama's reported net worth in 2007 was $1.3 million. In 2018 their net worth is estimated at $40 million.

Any president that comes out of office $40 million richer than when they entered the office on a $400,000 salary should be investigated immediately. There should even be a law that prevents a president from making any other type of income while serving.

FACT #80:

In 2009 Obama won the Nobel Peace Prize for his "extraordinary efforts to strengthen international diplomacy and cooperation between peoples." In 2016 he dropped 26,171 bombs around the world.

It's ironic he won the Nobel Peace Prize for "strengthening international diplomacy" when he was factually the weakest foreign policy president in the history of our country:

"There's a red line in the sand, don't cross it." Syria proceeds to piss on the red line. Obama does nothing.

He was like the parent at a party with their 5-year-old bouncing off the walls making empty threat after empty threat, and then to shut the kid up he rewards them with a pallet of cash, which only works for a few minutes and then the kid is bouncing off the walls again. Worst foreign policy president in history. Not to mention his bomb dropping alone was not so "peaceful."

Obama also won this prize for "cooperation between peoples." In my short 28 years of life, I know for a fact that cooperation between peoples is at an all-time low because of Obama's tenure. He was a symbol of unity: a man that was half white and half black. Instead of uniting peoples, his tenure has brought our country's relations to an extremely divisive state.

FACTS #81, 82 & 83:

Under Obama, the national debt nearly doubled from $10.6 trillion to $19.9 trillion.

Under Obamacare, family health plans rose from $12,680 in 2008 to $18,142 in 2016.

In 2009, 33,490,000 people received food stamps. In 2016 there were 44,219,123 people on food stamps.

According to statistics, Americans were WAY worse off economically after Obama's term than when he came to power. Numbers do not lie. This is what happens when you try and convert to a socialist system; rising debt, increased consumer cost, and increased dependency on some who were once independent. Why on earth would anyone want this for their country and its citizens?

FACT #84:

Murders in Chicago vs. American casualties in Iraq and Afghanistan since 2001:

Chicago = 7,916 deaths

Iraq = 4,504 deaths

Afghanistan = 2,384 deaths

Obama began serving as an Illinois state Senator in 1997. A man that was supposedly Nobel Peace prize caliber let his home state and city of Chicago turn into a war zone. Why did he do nothing when the city desperately needed leadership?

ON THE CLINTONS

FACT #85:

From 2001-2015, the Clintons made nearly $240 million as public servants.

    The Clinton's have rigged the system to work in their favor. They have committed many questionable dealings, in the name of greed, and all while serving in some form or another as "public servants." Most of this money supposedly came from "speaking" events. What a great laundering tool. You can "speak" to any group of people for any set amount of money you'd like. While old Bill is off collecting the "speaking" money, Hillary is in office trying to make *special* deals and work her way up to the highest office of power in the world.

    Too bad 2016 didn't fare so well for two of the most corrupt people on the history of the planet. The worst part is that it's so transparent that people in the future are going to have a hard time believing it.

FACT #86:

Bill Clinton put a cigar up a woman's vagina in the oval office, literally and figuratively.

"But Donald Trump supposedly had sex with a porn star years before ever running for office."

The hypocrisy is staggering. Bill Clinton has sex with an intern, while married, while the President and the left still praise him. That's not even the beginning of his promiscuity. There are women lined up around the corner trying to tell their story of Bill Clinton, but nobody listens, which is funny now that the #MeToo movement is in full swing; putting men to shame with zero physical evidence. There is physical evidence with Bill (DNA on the dress). If you have never read the Starr Report, get on it. By the way, Hillary chastised these women and defended her husband's behavior. Doesn't seem very supportive of women, does it?

FACTS #87A & B:

Richard Nixon deleted 18 minutes of audio recordings and was forced to resign.

Hillary Clinton deleted 30,000 emails after *a subpoena and nothing happened.*

If you haven't figured it out, our next book will detail the 10 million examples of leftist hypocrisy. The Democrats threatened to impeach a Republican president and forced him to resign over 18 minutes of deleted audio. Hillary deleted more than 30,000 emails, and she was still allowed to run. Either I'm missing something here, or supporters of the left are deliberately ignorant or sorely misinformed. This is not okay, not only because there is information requested by the FBI that is missing, but because the court *ordered* Hillary to turn over the information and she threw up a middle finger to the courts ... AND NOTHING HAPPENED!

The worst part for me was seeing James Comey come out in his news conference and basically say, "Yea, she's guilty, but we're not going to charge her. Shame on her for being careless though."

Truly astonishing.

FACT #88:

96% of all campaign contributions from journalists went to Hillary Clinton.

The media is not biased though. Not in any sense of the word. Nope. They are completely objective and don't ever lean to one political party.

FACT #89:

Hillary Clinton spent and lost $1.2 billion on her campaign.

Nobody wants to see so much money get flushed down the toilet, but in this case, I think I speak for everyone who has their eyes open to the crimes of the Clintons when I say that I couldn't be happier to see this money wasted. If it was any indication of how efficient our economy would run, then we definitely made the right choice in Trump. Not to mention, what a horrible thing to be remembered for, which is a good thing since I hope she goes down in history as one of the biggest villains to ever set foot in the political arena because she is.

ON US EDUCATION

FACT #90:

A survey of Harvard professors says 83.16% identify as Liberal, 1.6% as Conservative.

Harvard will produce (as it always has) future Senators, Representatives, Supreme Court Justices and even Presidents. Those future leaders will be exposed to left-leaning ideas in the most impressionable years of their life while in college. How will their impressionable minds know any different when they aren't being taught any other ideas besides liberal ones? You are the sum of what you are surrounded by, and when immersed in a breeding ground of liberal ideologies, that is what you will become.

Let's take a step back and note that this is the common theme across the board in our universities. That being the case, other impressionable minds are being infused with liberal ideology at other schools. These future voters will be voting the Harvard students into office. The incredible disparity in ideologies of professors at universities makes for the perfect indoctrination and vote-manufacturing machine, and it explains why many people in their 20's and 30's are so left-leaning today.

On another note, the left preaches diversity, but when it comes to diversity of thought, specifically political philosophy, they throw that talking point out the window. Once again proving that they don't care about diversity at all.

FACT #91:

Just 7% of journalists identify as Republicans.

This goes back to the campaign contributions from journalists to Hillary in 2016. To me, that shows how indoctrinating our country's college system is. With people our age breaking into careers such as journalism, the number of journalists who identify as Republican continues to drop because of the ideas colleges have infused into impressionable minds.

To spout the notion that the media is not biased is a lie and is becoming more apparent to the American people every day. This is another objective fact that proves they are biased beyond their undeniably slanted reporting and they have rightfully earned the name "Fake News."

FACT #92:

NYC spends over $24,109 a year per public school student, yet 72% aren't proficient at reading, and 72% aren't proficient at math.

This stat is sad more than anything else. It teaches us a lot as well. It tells us that we can throw as much money as we want at trying to educate kids, but there are obviously other factors that come into play when kids learn, not just the amount of resources they have. Do they have both parents at home? Are the teachers of the caliber and quality necessary for a successful school year? Are the teachers themselves being benchmarked? And if the quality of the teacher is in question and they are in fact receiving insufficient teaching, are the teachers held accountable?

The left's solution to bad education is more money. It seems that is their solution to every issue. Money can solve a lot of problems and help with others, but it can't create a good teacher, and it can't make a kid want to learn.

FACT #93:

In 2016, US Teacher's Unions spent a record in political donations; $33.2 million. 93% of the money given to candidates went to Democrats.

To be fair, you should vote for who is going to give you the most funding right? It's the same thing as Lyndon B Johnson's enslavement idea with welfare. If someone is offering you money for free, and all you have to do is check a box on a ballot for them, most people are going to check that box. Teacher's Unions know they are going to not only get tens of thousands of dollars per student, but they are also going to get job security, take for example teachers in California (on to fact #94).

FACT #94:

There are 275,000 teachers in California, and they all have better odds of getting struck by lightning than they do of getting fired. Only 2.2 (yes, two point two, not a percent) teachers a year are fired for being a horrible teacher.

That is one of the most disgusting examples of how much power the unions have today.

TWO TEACHERS FIRED!?

I'll tell you right now that of the 30-ish teachers I had in high school there were more than two that should have been fired for being awful teachers. The arrogance exuded by several of them because they had tenure was noticeable even by the 18-year-old idiot that I was. I actually remember an AP class I took where we received such awful instruction that almost 90% of the class scored 1's on the AP test (If you're not familiar they score it 1-6, 1 being the lowest possible score, if you get a 4 most colleges will give you credit for the class). This is unacceptable, especially considering I got an A in that same course the next year, my Freshman year, at college.

Because of unions, teachers can literally sit there, say nothing or play on their computer and never get fired. It's abhorrent, and anyone with a child in public school should demand teacher's unions have powers taken away, or they may get a teacher that should have been fired ten years ago. Take responsibility for your child's education and the curriculum that is being taught to your children today.

ON GLOBAL WARMING/ POLLUTION

FACTS #95A & B:

Mars has ice caps that are melting.

There are no trucks on Mars.

"Conservatives don't believe in global warming!" You hear that all the time on this issue. You never hear, "Conservatives question the cause of global warming and that humans may not be it."

The latter is where most conservatives I know sit, and they should. Most data proves that the earth is warming, and conservatives don't deny these facts. Sometimes we question the source of those facts. If you remember, temperature statistics have been skewed by scientists on several occasions so they could keep their funding (see sources). It is a fact that Mars has ice caps that are melting, and it is also true that there are no human-induced emissions on Mars.

What's causing the ice caps on Mars to melt? Could it be the same thing that is causing the earth to warm? Something to do with the sun? If so, are we in a natural cycle just like the patterns of earth's past have shown with ice ages and temperature patterns?

Personally, it's sad to see so many self-loathing people in the world who mostly reside on the left side of the spectrum. Stop. Start looking at facts and quit hating yourself for things you did not do.

FACT #96:

95% of the plastic in our oceans comes from just TEN rivers. None of which are in the United States.

Surprise, surprise. The self-loathing, American-hating left tries to convince us that our country is the problem when it comes to everything, especially pollution. Facts don't lie. The US is very responsible in comparison to the rest of the world when it comes to taking care of our waste and pollution. Now, we can always make it better, and there's no reason not to because it is a good thing and we should take care of our home, but quit telling me I live in an evil place that is destroying our planet.

FACT #97:

After pulling out of the Paris Climate Accords, the US led the world in decreasing carbon emissions.

You mean to tell me that a law written on a piece of paper is not needed to get things done? How many times has this book proven that? The United States is leading the world in decreasing carbon emissions, and we are doing it on our own under leadership that knows how to get it done.

FACT #98:

Al Gore's Nashville estate uses 21x more energy than the average US home.

Democrat hypocrisy number 18,908,330 of 2018. This swamp rat has the nerve to preach lower consumption and less waste, but he consumes this much? That fact only accounts for the one estate, too! It doesn't include all of his private jet flying and luxurious living while traveling, or the other estates he has. If you let Al Gore's moral compass guide yours, especially when it comes to global warming, I highly recommend you take a long look at what he preaches vs. your beliefs.

ON ISLAM

FACT #99:

Islam is a religion, not a race.

I know white, black and middle Eastern people who follow Islam. Stop getting triggered when people criticize ideas such as a religion like Islam; it has nothing to do with the people that believe in it.

I have a Quran, I have read it, and it is full of ideas incompatible with western civilization. I was taken aback mostly by the repetitive line that "Christians and Jews are disbelievers." That is hammered home in that book over and over again, and it says Muslims should not associate with disbelievers. How is this peaceful? How can this cause humanity to, as the left virtue signals it, "coexist?"

FACT #100:

There have been over 33,500 attacks in the name of Islam since 9/11.

You can draw your own conclusions from this. I'm just giving you the facts that mainstream media does not deliver.

FACT #101:

Hitler said, "He alone, who owns the youth, gains the future."

I wanted to leave this thought for you as we near the end of the book, as it is becoming a cornerstone in the left's platform.

First, Conservatives and Trump supporters are blasted with rhetoric and name calling. Much of the name calling has something to do with "Nazi" or "fascist." It's ironic because fascism advocates a uniform way of doing things, and the left is the side that advocates a singular way of thinking, and if you don't you are then a "Nazi" or a "fascist." This uniform way of thinking that they promote is the very definition of fascism.

Second, when it comes to youth, stats in this book have proven that the left is doing it's best to "own the youth" with what is being taught in our schools by controlling who is teaching in our schools and deciding the curriculum of our schools. It is fair to say that they own the generation of Millennials (although I have hope that many are seeing through the facade).

Third, the left tries to own the youth in other various forms. When it comes to tragic school shootings, the left cries "we need to control guns better for the kids!" When it comes to immigration at the border, they desperately tried to pitch the story about "kids separated from their parents!" When it comes to funding programs, "our kids are our future, and we need this program." They are constantly trying to tug at our heartstrings by using kids to push their agendas.

Hitler saw the importance in owning the youth, and so do Liberals. We need to stand up and protect the minds of the impressionable because they are fed lies which will cause the demise of our nation.

CONCLUSION

The purpose of writing this book was to shed light on just a few of the non-debatable, jaw-dropping facts that we've come across during the short time we have spent studying politics together. We realize that one or two mind-blowing facts can spark someone's curiosity to dig deeper, research the truth for themselves, and ultimately change their life, as it did for both of us.

We have also learned that a passion for doing your research and finding the objective truth is something no longer taught in academia. You need to have the drive, energy, and willpower to do it for yourself. It's similar to that Old English proverb "You can lead a liberal to water, but you can't make them drink from it" (unless you put some Kool-Aid in there of course!). Ultimately, it is up to them and them alone to decide if they are thirsty for the knowledge or not. And unfortunately, that is the problem we are seeing with far too many people today—they are not thirsty enough to seek out the truth for themselves, even when served on a silver platter for them. They have become too accustomed to receiving their news and information from the mainstream media, government, politicians, social media, teachers, and anyone else they consider to be in a position of authority—without doing the fact-checking or research themselves. That is the sad reality we live in, and it is precisely why the epidemic of "fake news" is running rampant in America.

A lot of this boils down to simple psychology. The reason why most people, specifically liberals, have such a hard time accepting new information and changing their beliefs is cognitive dissonance. Changing their minds when presented with new evidence contrary to what they already believe makes them feel uncomfortable. Most of them are not ready to be intellectually challenged and have the illusions of their current reality shattered. It's the same reason why most people still believe 100% fruit juice is pure fruit juice. More often than not, they are emotionally immature and refuse to listen to anything that does not correlate directly to their current beliefs—this is known as confirmation bias. They would rather let their pride and ego get in the way of being corrected and feeling "stupid," especially if they are being corrected on social media or in a public setting. This proverb holds truer now than ever before—"correct a fool and he will hate you, correct a wise man and he will thank you."

Another quote that sums up our almost impossible task of educating the misinformed public goes as follows, "It is easier to fool someone than to convince them they have been fooled." The mainstream media has already planted the seeds of misinformation and has been doing so for many decades. But the advent of the internet and social media has helped level the playing field in this fight against psychological warfare. We are now capable of using our thumb to figure out most of the questions we have on any given day within a matter of seconds. Hollywood and the mainstream media no longer hold a monopoly on the news and entertainment industry. Instead of listening to cable media telling you how to think, people are crossing over to the Internet to find unbiased sources of news and information. And instead of listening to the Hollywood "elite" preach to us as if they are morally superior, people are heading over to YouTube to watch their favorite YouTubers.

Times are changing quickly, and many good things are happening in America thanks to President Trump and his America First policies. But some people may never get the chance to see that if they allow themselves to remain victims of the fake news media that desperately wants to keep us divided and fighting. Everybody is at a different stage of knowledge and enlightenment. Some people have been programmed harder than others by the media's deliberate attempt at spreading misinformation. So be kind to each other, focus on some of the positives, and keep spreading the truth to those who are willing to listen. Together we are stronger. Together we are more intelligent. And together we have the power and capability to do amazing things for our country, and this world never thought possible. We both wish you a life full of peace, love, and positivity. Thank you for taking the time to read our book, and God bless America!

RESOURCES

1. Carney, John. "How the Government Caused the Mortgage Crisis." Business Insider. 16 October 2009.
http://www.businessinsider.com/how-the-government-caused-the-mortgage-crisis-2009-10

Fact #1:
United States Equal Opportunity Commission. "The Equal Pay Act of 1963."
https://www.eeoc.gov/laws/statutes/epa.cfm

Fact #2:
United States Equal Opportunity Commision. "Equal Pay Act Charges (Charges Filed With EEOC) (includes concurrent charges with Title VII, ADEA, ADA, and GINA) FY 1997 - FY 2017."
https://www.eeoc.gov/eeoc/statistics/enforcement/epa.cfm
U.S. Census Bureau. "2010-2014 American Community Survey 5-Year Estimates."
https://factfinder.census.gov/faces/tableservices/jsf/pages/productview.xhtml?pid=ACS_14_5YR_DP05&src=pt

Fact #3:
Merline, John. "Gender Pay Gap? What About The Workplace Death Gap?" *Investor's Business Daily*. 03 April 2017.
https://www.investors.com/politics/commentary/how-come-nobody-talks-about-the-gender-workplace-death-gap/

Fact #4:
No Author. "Men Sentenced To Longer Prison Terms Than Women For Same Crimes, Study Says." *Huffington Post*. 11 September 2012.
https://www.huffingtonpost.com/2012/09/11/men-women-prison-sentence-length-gender-gap_n_1874742.html

Fact #5:
American Foundation for Suicide Prevention. "Suicide Statistics."
https://afsp.org/about-suicide/suicide-statistics/
Cancer.net Editorial Board. "Breast Cancer: Statistics." Cancer.Net. January 2018.
https://www.cancer.net/cancer-types/breast-cancer/statistics

Fact #6:
National Cancer Institute. "Cancer Stat Facts: Prostate Cancer."
https://seer.cancer.gov/statfacts/html/prost.html

Fact #7:
National Coalition Against Domestic Violence. "Statistics."
https://ncadv.org/statistics

Fact #8:
Family and Youth Services Bureau. "Getting Help With Domestic Violence." 01 October 2014.
https://www.acf.hhs.gov/fysb/resource/help-fv

Jarvie, Jenny. "It's hard for a guy to say, 'I need help.'" How shelters reach out to male victims of domestic violence." *LA Times*. 05 August 2017.
http://www.latimes.com/nation/la-na-male-domestic-violence-shelter-20170804-story.html

Fact #9:
National Football League. "2018 NFL Rulebook."
https://operations.nfl.com/the-rules/2018-nfl-rulebook/

Fact #10:
Marcus, John. "Why Men are the New College Minority." *The Atlantic*. 08 August 2017.
https://www.theatlantic.com/education/archive/2017/08/why-men-are-the-new-college-minority/536103/

Fact #11:
Scutti, Susan. "Sperm Counts of Western Men Plummeting, Analysis Finds." *CNN*. 25 July 2017.
https://www.cnn.com/2017/07/25/health/sperm-counts-declining-study/index.html

Fact #12:
Tumbokon, Karen. "Transgender Surgeries on the Rise in the US, Says Study." *Tech Times*. 04 March 2018
https://www.techtimes.com/articles/222273/20180304/transgender-surgeries-on-the-rise-in-the-us-says-study.htm

Fact #13:
Snopes. "Hillary Clinton: 'Marriage Is Always Between a Man and a Woman."
https://www.snopes.com/fact-check/hillary-clinton-marriage-is-always-between-a-man-and-a-woman/

Fact #14:
Bowers, Becky. "President Barack Obama's Shifting Stance on Gay Marriage." *Politifact*. 11 May 2012
http://www.politifact.com/truth-o-meter/statements/2012/may/11/barack-obama/president-barack-obamas-shift-gay-marriage/

Fact #15:
Carr, Flora. "This Is the Woman President Trump Wants to Be the First Female African-American Marine General." *Time Magazine*. 13 April 2018.
http://time.com/5237828/first-african-american-woman-general/
USA Today. "Gina Haspel: First Woman to Lead the CIA."
https://www.usatoday.com/picture-gallery/news/politics/2018/05/06/gina-haspel-first-woman-to-lead-the-cia/34632319/
Morrongiello, Gabby. "Conway Shatters Glass Ceiling as First Woman to Run a Successful Presidential Campaign." *Washington Examiner*. 10 November 2016.
https://www.washingtonexaminer.com/conway-shatters-glass-ceiling-as-first-woman-to-run-a-successful-presidential-campaign

Fact #16:
Kristof, Nicholas. "Some Inconvenient Gun Facts for Liberals." *New York Times*. 16 January 2016.
https://mobile.nytimes.com/2016/01/17/opinion/sunday/some-inconvenient-gun-facts-for-liberals.html?referer=

Fact #17:
G.R. "In New Orleans, Call 911 and Wait for an Hour." *The Economist*. 10 December 2015.
https://www.economist.com/blogs/democracyinamerica/2015/12/police-response-timesFact

#18:
Logic

Fact #19:
Statista. "Number of murder victims in the United States in 2016, by weapon."
https://www.statista.com/statistics/195325/murder-victims-in-the-us-by-weapon-used/

Fact #20:
Statista. "Number of murder victims in the United States in 2016, by weapon."
https://www.statista.com/statistics/195325/murder-victims-in-the-us-by-weapon-used/

Fact #21:
Armalite. "History over 60 years of Armalite!"
https://www.armalite.com/history/

Fact #22:
Hoyert, Donna L. & Xu, Jiaquan. "Deaths: Preliminary Data for 2011." National Vital Statistics Reports, Volume 61, Number 6. 10 October 2012.
https://www.cdc.gov/nchs/data/nvsr/nvsr61/nvsr61_06.pdf

Fact #23:
Foundation For Economic Education. "Defensive Gun Use is More Than Shooting Bad Guys." 27 February 2018
https://fee.org/articles/defensive-gun-use-is-more-than-shooting-bad-guys/

Fact #24:
Hiskey, Daven. "Gun "Silencers" Don't Make Them Anywhere Near Silent." Today I Found Out. 04 November 2010.
http://www.todayifoundout.com/index.php/2010/11/gun-silencers-dont-make-them-anywhere-near-silent/
SilencerCo. "Silencer Ownership."
https://silencerco.com/suppressed/

Fact #25:
Newton's first law of motion.

Fact #26:
Koenigsberg, Richard A. "Nations Kill a lot of People." Library of Social Science.
https://www.libraryofsocialscience.com/newsletter/posts/2015/2015-06-18-RAK.html

Fact #27:
CNN Library. "Tiananmen Square Fast Facts." *CNN*. 27 May 2018.
https://www.cnn.com/2013/09/15/world/asia/tiananmen-square-fast-facts/index.html

Fact #28:
World Atlas. "Murder Rate by Country."
https://www.worldatlas.com/articles/murder-rates-by-country.html
Kopel, David & Harinam, Vincent. "In the wake of a gun ban, Venezuela sees rising homicide rate." *The Hill*. 19 April 2018.
http://thehill.com/opinion/campaign/383968-in-the-wake-of-a-gun-ban-venezuela-sees-rising-homicide-rate
Specht, Paul. "Does America Own 42 Percent of the World's Guns?" Politifact. 05 March 2018.
https://www.politifact.com/north-carolina/statements/2018/mar/05/pricey-harrison/does-america-have-42-percent-worlds-guns/

Fact #29 & #30:
Sanders, Katie. "Viral, flawed post compares Honduras, Switzerland on gun laws and homicide rates." *Politifact*. 30 September 2015.
https://www.politifact.com/punditfact/statements/2015/sep/30/viral-image/viral-flawed-post-compares-honduras-switzerland-gu/

Fact #31:
Spillett, Richard. "Knife crimes soars by more than a fifth across England and Wales driven by weapons epidemic in London - where the murder rate increased by 44%." *Daily Mail*. 26 April 2018.
http://www.dailymail.co.uk/news/article-5659471/London-murder-rate-soars-44-cent-knife-crime-one-fifth-year.html
Casciani, Dominic. "Gun Control and Ownership Laws in the UK." *BBC*. 02 November 2010.
https://www.bbc.com/news/10220974

Fact #32:
Crime Prevention Research Center. "Comparing Death Rates from Mass Public Shootings and Mass Public Violence in the US and Europe." 23 June 2015.
https://crimeresearch.org/2015/06/comparing-death-rates-from-mass-public-shootings-in-the-us-and-europe/

Fact #33:
Wikipedia. "Mass Shootings in the United States."
https://en.wikipedia.org/wiki/Mass_shootings_in_the_United_States

Fact #34:
Wikipedia. "List of School Massacres by Death Tolls."
https://en.wikipedia.org/wiki/List_of_school_massacres_by_death_toll

Fact #35:
Palmieri, Jacob. "Study: 75% of mass shooters choose handguns to commit mass shootings." Palmieri Report. 31 May 2018.
https://thepalmierireport.com/study-75-of-mass-shooters-choose-handguns-to-commit-mass-shootings/

Fact #36:
Crime Prevention Research Center. "Mass Public Shootings keep occurring in Gun-Free Zones: 97.8% of attacks since 1950." 15 June 2018.
https://crimeresearch.org/2018/05/more-misleading-information-from-bloombergs-everytown-for-gun-safety-on-guns-analysis-of-recent-mass-shootings/

Fact #37:
Meckler, Mark. "Of the 27 Deadliest Mass Shooters, 26 of Them Had One Thing in Common." Patheos. 20 February 2018.
http://www.patheos.com/blogs/markmeckler/2018/02/27-deadliest-mass-shooters-26-one-thing-common/
Hasson, Peter. "Guess Which Mass Murderers Came From A Fatherless Home." *The Federalist*. 14 July 2015
http://thefederalist.com/2015/07/14/guess-which-mass-murderers-came-from-a-fatherless-home/

Fact #38:
National Center for Fathering. "The Consequences of Fatherlessness."
http://www.fathers.com/statistics-and-research/the-consequences-of-fatherlessness/

Fact #39:
Bruenig, Matt. "The Child Poverty Rate For Married Families Is Extremely High." Demos. 03 March 2015.
https://www.demos.org/blog/3/3/15/child-poverty-rate-married-families-extremely-high

Fact #40:
Duckworth, Lorna. "Rates of self harm higher for children from broken homes." *Independent*. 18 August 2001.
https://www.independent.co.uk/news/uk/this-britain/rates-of-self-harm-higher-for-children-from-broken-homes-5363916.html
The Heritage Foundation. "The War on Poverty: 50 Years of Failure." 23 September 2014.
https://www.heritage.org/marriage-and-family/commentary/the-war-poverty-50-years-failure

Fact #41 an #42:
National Center for Fathering. "The Extent of Fatherlessness."
http://www.fathers.com/statistics-and-research/the-extent-of-fatherlessness/

Fact #43:
Jacobson, Louis. "CNN's Don Lemon says more than 72 percent of African-American births are out of wedlock." *Politifact*. 29 July 2013.
https://www.politifact.com/truth-o-meter/statements/2013/jul/29/don-lemon/cnns-don-lemon-says-more-72-percent-african-americ/

Fact #44:
FBI, Criminal Justice Information Services Division. "Crime in the United States 2013."
https://ucr.fbi.gov/crime-in-the-u.s/2013/crime-in-the-u.s.-2013/tables/table-43

Fact #45:
Sherman, Amy. "An Updated look at Statistics on Black on Black Murders." *Politifact*. 21 May 2015.
https://www.politifact.com/florida/article/2015/may/21/updated-look-statis-tics-black-black-murders/

Fact #46:
Riley, Jason L. "The Real Crime Problem Doesn't Make Much News." *Wall Street Journal*. 10 January 2017.
https://www.wsj.com/articles/the-real-crime-problem-doesnt-make-much-news-1484093102

Fact #47:
O'Donnell, Dan. "The Myth of the Republican-Democrat 'Switch.'" The Dan O'Donnell Show. 01 May 2018.
https://newstalk1130.iheart.com/featured/common-sense-central/content/2018-05-01-the-myth-of-the-republican-democrat-switch/

Fact #48:
Biography. "Robert C. Byrd."
https://www.biography.com/people/robert-c-byrd-579660

Fact #49:
Blake, Andrew. "Klan Leader Claims KKK has given $20k to Clinton Campaign." *Washington Times*. 26 April 2016.
https://www.washingtontimes.com/news/2016/apr/26/klan-leader-claims-kkk-has-given-20k-clinton-campa/

Fact #50:
Wikipedia. "Grand Wizard."
https://en.wikipedia.org/wiki/Grand_Wizard#Grand_Wizards_or_Imperial_Wizards

Fact #51:
Southern Poverty Law Center. "Ku Klux Klan."
https://www.splcenter.org/fighting-hate/extremist-files/ideology/ku-klux-klan

Fact #52:
History. "House Passes 13th Amendment."
https://www.history.com/this-day-in-history/house-passes-the-13th-amendment
Blanton, John. "Quick History Lesson." 17 November 2013.
https://skeptic78240.wordpress.com/2013/11/17/quick-history-lesson/
USA Today. "Black Voters Would be Wise to go Republican: Your Say." USA Today. 23 August 2016.
https://www.usatoday.com/story/opinion/2016/08/23/black-voters-wise-go-republican-say/89221394/

Fact #53:
USA Today. "Black Voters Would be Wise to go Republican: Your Say." USA Today. 23 August 2016.
https://www.usatoday.com/story/opinion/2016/08/23/black-voters-wise-go-republican-say/89221394/

Facet #54:
USA Today. "Black Voters Would be Wise to go Republican: Your Say." USA Today. 23 August 2016.
https://www.usatoday.com/story/opinion/2016/08/23/black-voters-wise-go-republican-say/89221394/

Fact #55:
Stewart, Alicia W. & Escobedo, Tricia. "What you might not know about the 1964 Civil Rights Act." *CNN*. 10 April 2014.
https://www.cnn.com/2014/04/10/politics/civil-rights-act-interesting-facts/index.html

Fact #56:
History, Art & Archives, United States House of Representatives. "Revels, Hiram Rhodes."
http://history.house.gov/People/Listing/R/REVELS,-Hiram-Rhodes-(R000166)/

Fact #57:
Biography. "Carol Moseley Braun."
https://www.biography.com/people/carol-moseley-braun-205626

Fact #58:
Mahdawi, Arwa. "Harvard Sued for Alleged Discrimination Against Asian Americans." *The Guardian*. 15 June 2018.

https://www.theguardian.com/education/2018/jun/15/harvard-sued-discrimination-against-asian-americans

Fact #59:
Strickland, Ashley. "Planned Parenthood: Fast Facts and Revealing Numbers." *CNN*. 01 August 2017
https://www.cnn.com/2015/08/04/health/planned-parenthood-by-the-numbers/index.html
Planned Parenthood. "2014-15 Annual Report."
https://www.plannedparenthood.org/files/2114/5089/0863/2014-2015_PPFA_Annual_Report_.pdf
Ye Hee Lee, Michelle. "For Planned Parenthood abortion stats, '3 percent' and '94 percent' are both misleading." *Washington Post*. 12 August 2015.

https://www.washingtonpost.com/news/fact-checker/wp/2015/08/12/for-planned-parenthood-abortion-stats-3-percent-and-94-percent-are-both-misleading/?utm_term=.8e7a6842ef27

Fact #60:
Prestigiacomo, Amanda. "How Much Cash Did Planned Parenthood Clear Last Year? The Answer Will Disgust You." *Daily Wire*. 19 December 2016.
https://www.dailywire.com/news/11723/how-much-cash-did-planned-parenthood-clear-last-amanda-prestigiacomo

Fact #61:
Live Action. "Debunking Planned Parenthood's 3% Abortion Myth."
https://www.liveaction.org/learn/3percent/

Fact#62:
Caruba, Lauren. "Cynthia Meyer says more black babies are aborted in New York City than born." Politifact. 25 November 2015.
https://www.politifact.com/texas/statements/2015/nov/25/cynthia-meyer/cynthia-meyer-says-more-black-babies-are-aborted-n/

Fact #63:
Patel, Jugal K. "After Sandy Hook, More Than 400 People Have Been Shot in Over 200 School Shootings." New York Times. 15 February 2018
https://www.nytimes.com/interactive/2018/02/15/us/school-shootings-sandy-hook-parkland.html
Abort73. "U.S. Abortion Statistics."
http://abort73.com/abortion_facts/us_abortion_statistics/

Fact #64:
Berg, Nate. "Muting the Freeway." Medium.com. 30 November 2014
https://medium.com/re-form/muting-the-freeway-e18ee195bd38

Fact #65:
Wikipedia. "Hungarian Border Barrier."
https://en.wikipedia.org/wiki/Hungarian_border_barrier

Fact #66:
Goldberg, Eleanor. "80% Of Central American Women, Girls Are Raped Crossing Into The U.S." *Huffington Post*. 06 December 2017
https://www.huffingtonpost.com/2014/09/12/central-america-migrants-rape_n_5806972.html

Fact #67:
Woody, Christopher. "The US and Mexico may be teaming up to fight heroin, but the enemy is tougher than it appears." *Business Insider.* 16 May 2017.
https://www.businessinsider.com/us-mexico-heroin-eradication-efforts-problems-2017-5

Fact #68:
Main, Douglas. "Heroin Addiction Costs US More than $50 Billion per year." *Newsweek.* 17 June 2017
https://www.newsweek.com/heroin-addiction-costs-us-more-50-billion-year-626983

Fact #69:
Fox News, "New data reveals US faces legal immigration crisis." 21 May 2018.
http://www.foxnews.com/transcript/2018/05/21/new-data-reveals-us-faces-legal-immigration-crisis.html

Fact #70:
Yee, Vivian. "Thousands of Federal Inmates Are in the U.S. Illegally, Administration Says." *New York Times.* 21 December 2017.
https://www.nytimes.com/2017/12/21/us/undocumented-immigrants-crimes.html
Prison Bureau. "Annual Determination of Average Cost of Incarceration." *Federal Register.* 19 July 2016.
https://www.federalregister.gov/documents/2016/07/19/2016-17040/annual-determination-of-average-cost-of-incarceration
Federation for American Immigration Reform. "Criminal Aliens." May 2016.
https://www.fairus.org/issue/societal-impact/criminal-aliens

Fact #71:
Aizenman, Nurith. "Mexicans in the US are Sending Home More Money Than Ever." NPR. 10 February 2017.
https://www.npr.org/sections/goatsandsoda/2017/02/10/514172676/mexicans-in-the-u-s-are-sending-home-more-money-than-ever

Fact #72:
O'Brien, Matt & Raley, Spencer. "The Cost of Illegal Immigration on US Tax Payers." Federation for American Immigration Reform. 27 September 2017.
https://fairus.org/issue/publications-resources/fiscal-burden-illegal-immigration-united-states-taxpayers

Fact #73:
Reilly, Katie. "Sesame Street reaches out to 2.7 million American children with an incarcerated parent." Pew Research Center. 21 June 2013
http://www.pewresearch.org/fact-tank/2013/06/21/sesame-street-reaches-out-to-2-7-million-american-children-with-an-incarcerated-parent/
Lind, Dara. "New statistics: the government is separating 65 children a day from parents at the border." Vox. 19 June 2018.
https://www.vox.com/2018/6/19/17479138/how-many-families-separated-border-immigration

Fact #74:
Gomez, Alan. "Report: More than Half of Immigrants on Welfare." *USA Today.* 02 September 2015
https://www.usatoday.com/story/news/nation/2015/09/01/immigrant-welfare-use-report/71517072/

Camarota, Steven A. "Welfare Use by Immigrant and Native Households." Center for Immigrant Studies. 10 September 2015
https://cis.org/Report/Welfare-Use-Immigrant-and-Native-Households

Fact #75:
White House. "Remarks by Vice President Pence at U.S. Immigration and Customs Enforcement." 06 July 2018.
https://www.whitehouse.gov/briefings-statements/remarks-vice-president-pence-u-s-immigration-customs-enforcement/

Fact #76:
Totenberg, Nina. "Supreme Court Upholds Controversial Ohio Voter-Purge Law." NPR. 11 June 2018.
https://www.npr.org/2018/06/11/618870982/supreme-court-upholds-controversial-ohio-voter-purge-law

Fact #77:
United States Census Bureau. "Frequently Asked Questions."
https://www.census.gov/population/apportionment/about/faq.html

Fact #78:
Bill: Clinton Whitehouse Archives. "New Community - Immigration."
https://clintonwhitehouse1.archives.gov/White_House/Publications/html/briefs/iii-7.html
Chuck: The Day. "Democrats Forget Own History on Immigration." 27 June 2018.
https://www.theday.com/article/20180627/OP02/180629441
Obama: Benson, Guy. "Flashback Video: Here's Barack Obama Sounding Kind of Like ... Donald Trump on Illegal Immigration." Townhall. 11 January 2018.
https://townhall.com/tipsheet/guybenson/2018/01/11/flashback-video-watch-obama-soundingkind-of-like-trump-on-immigration-n2432830
Hillary: YouTube. "Hillary 2014 ... Just Because Your Child Gets Across The Border ... That Doesn't Mean The Child Gets To Stay." 09 September 2017.
https://www.youtube.com/watch?v=aydFRXW0DT8

Fact #79:
Mikkelson, David. "Net Worth of Presidents." Snopes. 28 December 2017.
https://www.snopes.com/fact-check/net-worths-of-presidents/
Mavadiya, Madhvi. "What Is Barack Obama's Net Worth." *Daily Mail*. 27 March 2018.
http://www.dailymail.co.uk/news/article-5549343/What-Barack-Obamas-net-worth.html
Alexander, Dan. "How Barack Obama Has Made $20 Million Since Arriving In Washington." *Forbes*. 20 January 2017. https://www.forbes.com/sites/danalexander/2017/01/20/how-barack-obama-has-made-20-million-since-arriving-in-washington/#302e0ebe5bf0

Fact #80:
Benjamin, Medea. "America dropped 26,171 bombs in 2016. What a bloody end to Obama's reign." *The Guardian*. 09 January 2017.
https://www.theguardian.com/commentisfree/2017/jan/09/america-dropped-26171-bombs-2016-obama-legacy
Nobel Prize. "The Nobel Peace Prize for 2009."
https://www.nobelprize.org/nobel_prizes/peace/laureates/2009/press.html

Fact #81:
Watson, Kathryn. "Under Trump's Watch, National Debt Tops $21 Trillion for First Time Ever." *CBS News*. 17 March 2018.
https://www.cbsnews.com/news/under-donald-trump-national-debt-tops-21-trillion-for-first-

time-ever/

Fact #82:
Tuttle, Brad. "Here's What's Happened to Health Care Costs in America in the Obama Years." *Time*. 04 October 2016
http://time.com/money/4503325/obama-health-care-costs-obamacare/

Fact #83:
Rodriguez, Katherine. "Under Obama, 10.7 Million More Use Food Stamps — A 32 Percent Jump." *Breitbart*. 27 December 2016
https://www.breitbart.com/big-government/2016/12/27/under-obama-10-7-million-more-use-food-stamps-a-32-percent-jump/

Fact #84:
McCarthy, Niall. "Homicides In Chicago Eclipse U.S. Death Toll In Afghanistan And Iraq [Infographic]." *Forbes*. 08 September 2016.
https://www.forbes.com/sites/niallmccarthy/2016/09/08/homicides-in-chicago-eclipse-u-s-death-toll-in-afghanistan-and-iraq-infographic/#cf9e04a7d754

Fact #85:
Alexander, Dan. "How Barack Obama Has Made $20 Million Since Arriving In Washington." *Forbes*. 20 January 2017.
https://www.forbes.com/sites/danalexander/2017/01/20/how-barack-obama-has-made-20-million-since-arriving-in-washington/#5136286e5bf0

Fact #86:
The Starr Report. "The Starr Report." *Washington Post*.
https://www.washingtonpost.com/wp-srv/politics/special/clinton/icreport/icreport.htm

Fact #87:
Kopel, David. "The missing 18 1/2 minutes: Presidential destruction of incriminating evidence." *Washington Post*. 16 June 2014.
https://www.washingtonpost.com/news/volokh-conspiracy/wp/2014/06/16/the-missing-18-12-minutes-presidential-destruction-of-incriminating-evidence/
Carroll, Lauren. "Donald Trump says Hillary Clinton deleted 33,000 emails after getting a subpoena." *Politifact*. 09 October 2016.
https://www.politifact.com/truth-o-meter/statements/2016/oct/09/donald-trump/donald-trump-says-hillary-clinton-deleted-33000-em/

Fact #88:
Bahler, Kristen. "Journalists Have Donated Nearly $400K to Hillary Clinton's Campaign." *Time*. 17 October 2016.
http://time.com/money/4533729/hillary-clinton-journalist-campaign-donations/

Fact #89:
Fredericks, Bob. "Hillary Clinton's losing campaign cost a record $1.2B." *New York Post*. 09 December 2016.
https://nypost.com/2016/12/09/hillary-clintons-losing-campaign-cost-a-record-1-2b/

Fact #90:
Wang, Lucy & Xu, Luke. "Eighty-Eight Percent of Surveyed Harvard Faculty Believe Trump Has Done a 'Very Poor' Job as President." *The Crimson*. 02 May 2018.
https://www.thecrimson.com/article/2018/5/2/faculty-survey-part-2/

Fact #91:
Cillizza, Chris. "Just 7 percent of journalists are Republicans. That's far fewer than even a decade ago." *Washington Post*. 06 May 2014.
https://www.washingtonpost.com/news/the-fix/wp/2014/05/06/just-7-percent-of-journalists-are-republicans-thats-far-less-than-even-a-decade-ago/

Fact #92:
Jeffrey, Terence P. "No. 1: NYC Public Schools Spent $24,109 Per Pupil; But 72% Not Proficient in Reading, 72% Not Proficient in Math." *CNS News*. 21 May 2018.
https://www.cnsnews.com/news/article/terence-p-jeffrey/no-1-nyc-public-schools-spent-24109-pupil-72-not-proficient-reading

Fact #93:
Fox News. "By the numbers: Teachers union political contributions in 2016." 17 January 2017.
http://www.foxnews.com/politics/2017/01/17/by-numbers-teachers-union-political-contributions-in-2016.html

Fact #94:
The Editorial Board. "Firing Tenured Teacher: Our View." *USA Today*. 16 June 2014.
https://www.usatoday.com/story/opinion/2014/06/16/teacher-tenure-los-angeles-vergara-editorials-debates/10640909/

Fact #95:
NASA. "Mars is Melting." 07 August 2003.
https://www.nasa.gov/vision/universe/watchtheskies/8aug_mars_melting.html
Booker, Christopher. "The fiddling with temperature data is the biggest science scandal ever." *The Telegraph*. 07 February 2015.
https://www.telegraph.co.uk/news/earth/environment/globalwarming/11395516/The-fiddling-with-temperature-data-is-the-biggest-science-scandal-ever.html

Fact #96:
Best, Shivali. "Shocking report reveals that 95% of plastic polluting the world's oceans comes from just TEN rivers including the Ganges and Niger." *Daily Mail*. 11 October 2017.
http://www.dailymail.co.uk/sciencetech/article-4970214/95-plastic-oceans-comes-just-TEN-rivers.html

Fact #97:
Zanotti, Emily. "After Pulling Out Of Paris Climate Accords, U.S. Led The World In Decreasing Carbon Emissions Last Year." *Daily Wire*. 16 July 2018.
https://www.dailywire.com/news/33129/after-pulling-out-paris-climate-accords-us-led-emily-zanotti

Fact #98:
Chasmar, Jessica. "Al Gore's Nashville estate expends 21 times more energy a year than typical U.S. home, study says." *Washington Times*. 02 August 2017.
https://www.washingtontimes.com/news/2017/aug/2/al-gores-nashville-estate-expends-21-times-more-en/

Fact #99:
Logic.

Fact #100:
Religion of Peace. "Islamic Terrorists Have Carried out 33,000+ Deadly Terror Attacks since 9/11."
https://www.thereligionofpeace.com/

Fact #101:
Hafiz, Yasmine. "Bible School Uses Hitler Quote To Promote Education For Children." *Huffington Post*. 03 June 2014.
https://www.huffingtonpost.com/2014/06/03/bible-school-hitler-quote_n_5440205.html

ACKNOWLEDGEMENTS

A very special thank you to the following people who worked on this book with Dylan and I. Without them this book wouldn't exist and we can't thank them enough for the work they put into it and the guidance they provided us on our very first book.

Ben Garrison - Book cover Illustrator

Patti Fowler - Editor

Janelle Tepper - Proofreader

Thank you to the following people who have supported us throughout this process on social media and on our Patreon site. With the support we have received it makes it easy to wake up and keep pushing to spread our message! Thank you! Please check these amazing people out on their Twitter handles listed!

Lisa Kay Blackwell - @Lisa_Kay_71
Victoria Jenkins - @gringaloca11
Jacob Schneider - @jacobkschneider
Patrick's Mom
Skin Bag Becky - @SkinBag
Ruth in Texas - @IAmRuthless102
Gigi Johnston - @GJohnston2014
Daniel Wagalrich
Ricky L Smith - @NiceHarley
Reese Sagendorf
Tabitha Wright - @twright393
Samuel Thomas Nelson - @Samuel_Nelson
Christine Meyers - @Not Mater_Sammiches
Kyle King - @KyleKing212
Ben Squires - @Swytchback532
The Ethington Family
Men For America - @MenForAmerica1
Melissa Brown - @lisserlou47
Derek Fornof - @DFornof5827
Johnny Kratt
@joannarn4kids
Thomas J Gibson

Made in the USA
San Bernardino, CA
06 February 2020